ENEMIES

THE
PRESS

VS.

THE
AMERICAN
PEOPLE

PETER D'ABROSCA

Post Hill
PRESS

A BOMBARDIER BOOKS BOOK
An Imprint of Post Hill Press
ISBN: 978-1-64293-199-0
ISBN (eBook): 978-1-64293-200-3

Enemies:
The Press vs. The American People

Cover Design by Cody Corcoran

Post Hill Press
New York • Nashville
posthillpress.com

Published in the United States of America

For the righteously indignant.

TABLE OF CONTENTS

FOREWORD

If you're reading this book, there's a good chance you already know the media is, at the very least, not your friend. In fact, you're likely aware that the media has been stabbing you in the back right in front of your face. You know they've been pushing a one-sided agenda while only pretending to have your interests at heart, pretending to be objective, pretending to speak truth to power, pretending to be the one institution protecting our country from the brink of collapse.

We're all aware of this. But the evidence, when presented to us, is still shocking.

For my book, *The Scandalous Presidency of Barack Obama*, I not only detailed dozens of very real and serious scandals of the Obama administration but I also showed how the media ignored and downplayed every single one of them. That was, perhaps, the most scandalous aspect of it all. The media didn't speak truth to power when Barack Obama exceeded his constitutional authority, violated laws or covered up crimes, or even attacked the institution of the free press. Their *modus operandi* was to protect Barack Obama at all costs. They didn't deign to be objective when it came to covering America's first black president. With their help, Obama was elected to the highest office of the land (twice!) despite his radical agenda, lack of executive experience, and repeated abuses of power.

Compare that with how they've treated President Donald J. Trump. His media coverage is 90 percent negative—despite a more substantial record of accomplishment in two years than Obama had over eight. That Trump is doing a good job is irrelevant. The media's *modus operandi* is no longer to protect the president at all costs, but to take the president down.

But, the media's love for Obama and hate for Trump is just the tip of the media bias iceberg—there's so much more under the surface. In *Enemies: The Press vs. The American People*, Peter D'Abrosca tackles the entire iceberg, thoroughly exposing the media's dishonesty as they work tirelessly to destroy, not just Trump, but all things conservative. Peter tackles the issues in a forthright manner. Just as he does in his reporting at *Big League Politics*, Peter gives the mainstream a thorough beatdown, tackling the issue of media bias with humor and brutal honesty, calling them out for their B.S. Like Trump, Peter "tells it like it is."

Perhaps that's why it's no surprise that, like myself, Peter grew up in New England. We've both managed to survive the bluest of the blue areas on the map and come out conservative. We know what it's like to be surrounded by people who unquestioningly believe left-wing talking points. We know that the best way to fight back against the propaganda is to be ruthless. In this book, Peter is just that.

It should never be the objective of the media to protect a president because they agree with the president's policies. The first amendment exists as a check on the power of the government. For too long, the media has been acting like state-sponsored propaganda for the Democrat Party, shamelessly parroting left-wing talking points while acting bewildered whenever someone, particularly President Trump, doesn't appreciate their hard work. The evidence Peter presents in this book demonstrates conclusively that the mainstream media is nothing more than the public relations arm of the Democratic party.

Matt Margolis
Author of *Trumping Obama:*
How President Trump Saved Us From
Barack Obama's Legacy

CHAPTER 1

THE STATE OF THE MEDIA

In August of 2018 I attended an Antifa protest of the Silent Sam statue on the campus of the University of North Carolina at Chapel Hill as part of my duties as a national political reporter. The protest quickly turned into a violent riot, during which I was assaulted three times by masked Antifa thugs. I took a fairly serious blow to the head before Campus Police broke up the mob—and detained me instead of the raucous "anti-fascists" who were guilty of the assault.

After being hauled into an academic building crawling with a paramilitary brigade of State Troopers, being handcuffed, tossed against a wall, and searched while police blinded me with LED flashlights, I calmly explained that I was a reporter, showed my press credentials and the footage of my assault, and was released after police took a statement.

ABC11, a local news channel, covered the night's activities. They called it a "relatively peaceful" demonstration.[1] Perhaps it was, relative to the millions of dollars in property damage caused by hundreds of Antifas in Washington D.C.—including the burning of a Muslim man's limousine—during their riots after Trump's inauguration.[2] But why would the press excuse violence of that sort?

Later, *HuffPost* would write a hit piece on yours truly, blaming me for instigating the Antifa violence with my pesky reporting, and saying that there were no arrests until my "altercation" (a term used loosely to describe my questioning of black-clad, mask-wearing Antifas, which is my job) with the violent mob. I was also accused of "egging on" the mob. Further, *HuffPost* labeled me a "conspiracy theorist," and quoted some dopey PhD student—likely wasting her mid-twenties in the barren wasteland of academia—who insisted that I was a "sophisticated" fascist.[3] That part was sort of nice, considering it was the first time I have ever been called "sophisticated."

But the most striking part of the ordeal was not that ABC and *HuffPost* downplayed the radical nature and dangers of the far left, or that they failed to report on the assault of a fellow reporter at the hands of a violent leftist mob. Rather, it was their reaction hours earlier to two men who showed up at the rally hoisting a Confederate flag to counter protest on behalf of Silent Sam, which had been illegally toppled nearly a week earlier by brainwashed UNC halfwits.

Silent Sam was erected in 1913 by the Daughters of the Confederacy as a memorial to the Confederate soldiers who were students at UNC and took up arms to fight the Union Army during the Civil War. The atrocities committed by the Union Army were unspeakable. They included plundering, pillaging, and rape of anyone—white or black—who stood in the way of the storming Union troops. Often lost in the leftist rewrite of history is the fact that the Confederate Army was integrated. The statue honored the legacy of the young men who fought to protect their families before it was recklessly destroyed by lawless communists in the name of "equality." To them, the statue only represented "white supremacy," a notion surely taught by radical left-wing humanities professors who only teach because they lack the necessary skill set to work in private industry.

When the two men showed up to the campus, Confederate flag in tow, it was dusk. The rioting had yet to begin. Most of the participants were milling around, waiting for the cover of darkness.

The local mainstream press swarmed the men like a pack of hungry dogs, shoving cameras in their faces and taking endless pictures. There must have been thirty reporters who encircled the Southern men, gawking at them like they were rare zoo animals.

The press was bewildered. They simply could not believe their eyes. While dozens of purple-haired, eyebrow-pierced freaks wandered about like cast members in a B-roll zombie film, raggedly dressed in torn black clothing, masks covering their faces, waiting for the rioting to begin, the two average Joes sporting a Confederate flag instantly became the center of attention for the press.

Watching the press's reaction to the men was like peering into an alternate universe. In what world are Antifa rioters considered normal while ordinary Americans are ogled at like remnants from an ancient time? I could not help but wonder if that was the first time those members of the mainstream press corps had met anyone from Middle America. Were they aware that there are tens of millions of Americans just like those two men foisting the Confederate flag? Were they aware that men like that—hard working nine-to-fivers who are concerned with the direction of their dear nation—far outnumber the puny, albeit far louder, Antifa punks on college campuses? They were reporting the wrong news story!

By peacefully presenting the Stars and Bars, those two men triggered the Antifa ninnies. Eventually, a riot broke out that ended with three arrests that night, and several more arrests days later when myself and my colleagues pressed charges against those who were caught on our cameras assaulting us. Along with *HuffPost*, the rest of the mainstream press headlined their stories in defense of the rioters.

In a nutshell, this is the state of the mainstream press in the United States.

President Donald J. Trump has often called the press the "enemy of the American people," sparking feigned outrage among cable news talking heads like Rachel Maddow and Anderson Cooper. Trump is "attacking the free press," they screech on air. His rhetoric is "dangerous" and "authoritarian."

Cram it, losers.

As a member of the independent press—the truly free press that is not bought-and-paid-for by special interest groups, politicians, and lobbyists—I have yet to see an attack on the mainstream media that has not been warranted. The media's poor reputation has been well-earned. It has taken decades of consistent lying, misleading, and omission of facts in protection of their far-left narrative for them to rightly be deemed enemies of the American people. This country, after all, is and has always been a politically center-right nation. If not for constant propaganda spewed by the mainstream press, undoubtedly the mouthpiece for the Democratic National Committee, the far left's utterly insane political agenda would not have had a snowball's chance in hell of advancing as far as it has.

Trump was the first politician on a national stage with the nerve to call out their despicable behavior. He has trounced them over and over for their constant lies and embarrassed them continuously with impunity. Given his position as a president who is relatively unbeholden to the white glove Washington, D.C. donor class and their allies in the press, he has the latitude to say what everyone is thinking, which hurts the feelings of the CNN types who have never before had to face the wrath or righteous indignation of the ordinary American.

Though the press insists otherwise, Trump is not the cause of the distrust in media. He is the effect of distrust in media. Americans, by and large, are blessed with the inherent trait of common sense. Thankfully, that trait cannot be taught. If it could, academia would fail to teach it, like they do everything else, and Americans would be left high and dry, thinking that CNN is actually the guardian of all that is holy and truthful.

As early as 2012, only four in ten Americans trusted the news media. Only about half of the population trusted the press as far back as 1999.[4] The idea that Trump is discrediting the press is laughable. Ordinary Americans figured out that the news media was full of shit long before Trump even considered running for the highest office in the land. Trump simply confirmed their suspicions by providing daily examples from the "failing *New York Times*" and "fake news" CNN, NBC, and others and making a mockery out of them on a national stage at every turn. The press has roundly discredited itself in its haste to propagandize Americans with leftist talking points.

Despite the constant beating delivered by Trump, the mainstream press, particularly cable news, ought to be grateful for him. If not for Trump, they just might be six feet under by now. At least he provides them fodder to feed to the non-curious silver-haired crowd, which is the majority of their ever-dwindling audience.[5]

The numbers do not lie. President Trump has been a godsend for the middling media. All of the outrage directed at Trump by the media is completely manufactured. Before Trump, the press was teeter-tottering on the brink of irrelevance.

In fact, the most ubiquitous catch-22 of the Trump presidency has been his constant ability to destroy the mainstream press at every turn, while simultaneously making them relevant again. The cable news media ought to be kissing the feet of President Trump. They should worship the ground he walks on, considering that he saved their networks from near-certain demise. The news anchors who spend every waking moment demonizing Trump from their ivory towers ought to remember who built their towers in the first place. Certainly not their executives through any clever marketing schemes. It was not any cultural icon, Hollywood airhead, or boring milquetoast politician. It was the man who spent his entire life pre-politics building towers. Ironic, isn't it?

Remember when Rachel Maddow broke down in tears during her election night coverage? That was an Oscar-worthy performance better than anything Hollywood has produced in decades. And it was all an act.

"You're awake by the way," she said after the race was called for Trump. "You're not having a terrible, terrible dream. Also, you're not dead and you haven't gone to hell. This is your life now."[6]

It was a bit heavy on the melodrama, but Maddow nailed the crocodile tears. What she failed to mention was that in her blurry-eyed state, she was headed straight to the bank to cash in on her coverage of the president-elect.

In 2016, revenue for the cable news networks, including Maddow's MSNBC, jumped nearly $800 million from its total in 2015, from $3.9 billion to $4.7 billion, according to Pew Research. In the previous decade, the single largest revenue bump in a one-year timeframe was from 2007 to 2008, when the cable networks jumped about $400 million, from just over $2 billion to just over $2.4 billion.[7] The cable networks had never seen such a jump in revenue in a single year. They doubled their previous record on the back of none other than Donald J. Trump.

So, say it with me, Maddow: "Thank you, President Trump."

Nobody was tuning into cable news in 2015 or 2016 to watch anything except election coverage. It dominated the airwaves completely. And no one was tuning in to watch boring old Hillary Clinton meander her way through some scripted speech on healthcare for all, either. Certainly, nobody tuned in to watch her faint on September 11, 2016 and get chucked into a van by Secret Service like a rag doll, considering that they didn't cover it. That was at least interesting. But the mainstream press refused to cover Clinton's apparent health issues. The only time they gave it any attention at all was to call right wingers "conspiracy theorists" for bringing it up.[8]

On the contrary, everyone was tuning into cable news during that time frame to watch Donald Trump batter and bruise his way through the Republican primary field consisting of spineless weaklings like Ohio Governor John Kasich, Senator Marco Rubio (R-FL) and the anointed one, former Florida Governor Jeb! Bush. Now that was great TV! It had all the markings of a ratings-grabber. It was a compelling story about a political outsider. An underdog in D.C. politics committing blasphemy by speaking out on behalf of the everyman, willing to openly discuss issues that real people cared about, like illegal immigration and foreign governments doing their damnedest to put Americans out of work. Stack that up against scripted talking points handed down from consulting shops in D.C., parroted by empty suits like Rubio and Kasich, and later empty pantsuits like Clinton, and it's obvious who was hauling in the ratings.

"Tell us more about how you're a 'Reagan conservative,' Marco," said not one single truck driver from Iowa.

"You know, I'd really like to hear more about how Kasich's dad was a mailman," said no coal miner from West Virginia.

It was *all Trump*. Middle America did not care what out-of-touch D.C. focus groups said Middle America cared about. Middle America had heard all of the lines about "comprehensive immigration reform" (read: amnesty for millions of illegals) and "compassionate Conservatism" (also read: amnesty for millions of illegals) before. They wanted a wall, and they wanted jobs. Somehow, all of the focus groups managed to miss that.

So, the sixteen other Republican primary candidates floundered, simply becoming the minstrel show accompanied by the nobility that was Donald Trump. And, consequently, cable news ratings flourished.

In 2014, CNN averaged 515,000 viewers in primetime.[9] In 2015, they were up to an average of 712,000. Their most watched program of 2015, and in the *entire history of their network*, was the Republican primary debate in Simi Valley, California, which hauled in a stunning 23.1 million viewers.[10]

It may have been the most compelling event ever to grace cable television. Trump broke the matrix of American politics before the very eyes of the 23 million people watching on CNN. Nothing remotely as captivating had ever aired on cable news. Whether they thought he was a genius or a lunatic, Americans could not look away, and the cable news executives were seeing green.

The ratings only spiked from there. In 2016, CNN averaged more than 1.2 million viewers in prime time, a 76 percent increase from the prior year.[11] It was CNN's most-watched year in its thirty-six-year history to that point, until, on the back of Trump, it re-broke its own record in 2017.[12] In that year, CNN ranked in the top ten in cable news for the first time since 1995, coming in seventh.

All of those viewers turned into advertising revenue. And all that advertising revenue turned into paychecks, while all of those paychecks turned into fancy new clothes, cars, and homes for television executives and media personalities. And therein lies the motivation for all of the Trump hatred. Much of the audience that was sucked in during the 2016 campaign has hung around, though cable news ratings have taken a bit of a post-campaign dip.[13] But the networks know that the longer they keep up the facade that Trump is a no-good, unfit president and that they exist to serve as America's heroes, protecting us from his evil, the longer the gravy train will chug along.

That narrative is not based in reality. Historically, Trump is actually a quite popular president. His approval rating has hovered around 50 percent for most of his presidency, despite constant negative media coverage, which the president himself is keen on noting. But considering that it only takes about a million viewers in primetime for cable news to make a fortune, the press has taken a calculated risk. They know that by attracting just one million brainwash-able dullards to buy into their scheme, they are in the money. So, at the expense of the sacred trust of the vast majority of the American public, which consists of ordinary people, the press has actively decided to pander to the furthest-left audience out there—the apoplectic Trump haters who believe that Trump is *literally Hitler* and develop a nervous tick just thinking about his presidency. The other three hundred million plus Americans—the sane ones— are plain out of luck in the news department.

That is why the press does not recognize ordinary Americans when it sees them, like the Confederate Flag-bearing men at the Silent Sam riots. It is why they are completely out of touch with how normal people live, and what normal people believe. They have embedded themselves within the radical far left, and everyone who is not radically far left has become foreign to them. Between their existence in the leftist echo chamber of the newsroom, their fancy cocktail parties with other members of the leftist echo chamber, and their home lives in gated communities surrounded by more members of the leftist echo chamber, they have become completely isolated from anything remotely resembling an ordinary American.

During their endeavor to sell out the masses at the behest of the few, they have made up conspiracies about Russian "collusion," defended violence against Republicans, protected their own from racism and bigotry while slapping those labels onto the political right, told thousands of lies, twisted countless narratives, and engaged in an all-out propaganda war against a sitting president. Anyone who gets caught up in the alternate reality fabricated by the press is just a casualty of their money-grubbing ratings war.

Through all of that, the media still insists that they are our friend, and they feign outrage when the president challenges their undeserved authority. They are not our friend, and they are certainly not trustworthy. Of all their lies, those are the most serious and most-often repeated.

CHAPTER 2

WE'RE ALL GONNA DIE

President Trump was supposed to have killed us all at least a thousand times by now, according to the mainstream press. Fair assessments of Trump's policy proposals wouldn't keep the lights on at CNN, *The New York Times*, or *The Washington Post*. Good news does not sell advertisements. But apocalyptic predictions certainly do. For the purpose of making a buck, the mass media have insisted that Trump's presidency will ultimately lead to Americans occupying mass graves after a fiery death. The media have launched an all-out psychological warfare offensive against the public at large, which is just what a true enemy would do. But when Trump calls them out for overplaying their hands with hyperbolic rhetoric and doomsday prophecies—or calls them the enemy—they manage to slink their way onto the offensive with more fear mongering, telling Americans that Trump is a danger to the First Amendment and the "free press." This play garners sympathy, and thus more support from the liberal dupes who worship the ground walked upon by the likes of Rachel Maddow and

Jim Acosta. In turn, MSNBC and CNN sell more advertisements. Rinse, repeat, and rake in the cash. The enemy is a fickle bitch.

If I had a nickel for every time the mainstream press sounded the alarm about our certain death, I could retire today and sip margaritas on the beach until one of their doomsday predictions actually came true. The trustiest of such predictions promulgated in the press is climate change, a term used interchangeably with global warming because supposed "climate scientists" can't even figure out what's going on.

In 2006, failed Democratic presidential candidate Al Gore decided to try his hand in the movie-making business. He released "An Inconvenient Truth," which put the issue of climate change on the map, so to speak. Immediately thereafter, the mainstream press discovered that lecturing about how plastic bags would beget the certain death of mankind was a surefire moneymaker.

"If the vast majority of the world's scientists are right, we have just ten years to avert a major catastrophe that could send our entire planet into a tail-spin of epic destruction involving extreme weather, floods, droughts, epidemics and killer heat waves beyond anything we have ever experienced," Paramount, the film's distributor, said at the time of its release.[14]

The film grossed nearly $50 million worldwide,[15] which is plenty of money for Gore to refuel his not-so-eco-friendly private jet and travel the world peddling the famous line from his film—that "humanity is sitting on a ticking time bomb."

Since the movie's release, a hotly contested debate has ensued within the scientific community about the merits of climate change. In fact, nineteen thousand scientists and professionals signed a document called "the Oregon Petition," declaring that humans are not causing climate change. World renowned climatologist and award-winning NASA senior scientist for climate studies Roy W. Spencer says that there is no "consensus" in the scientific community that humans are causing climate change, and that climate change is most certainly not a "settled science."[16] The only scientific consensus, according to Spencer, is that the earth has warmed over the past century. Everything else—especially predictions of a doomsday caused by plastic straw usage—is pure speculation. Considering that the earth is billions of years old, us commoners might wonder whether a century's worth of data is an adequate sample size to lend credence to the idea that our planet is dying. To some, such a reasonable question might be called "common sense." To the political left, it is called "climate denial," for which one should be shunned by society.

From watching leftist cable news, one wouldn't know there was any debate on climate at all. Amateur climate scientists in mass media whose only credentials are degrees in journalism (a subject they still haven't even mastered) constantly bombard the American public with the idea that we are absolutely going to die, and that the only way to stop it is to vote Democrat. The news networks saw Gore's $50 million payday and immediately wanted to get a piece of the action.

Two particularly rough hurricanes hit the American southeast during late summer of 2018. Late summer is known as hurricane season to most in that region, given the proclivity for hurricanes at that time of year. At cable news networks, it's known as "Republicans are big dumb climate-denying idiots" season.

The media's duplicity is on full display when it comes to the way they interchangeably use the terms "weather" and "climate" while simultaneously chastising Republicans if they dare do the same.

When we have uncommonly cold winter days in America, the climate cult is sure to remind us that weather *absolutely does not equal* climate. But when it comes to hurricane season, all bets are off. When weather can be used by the leftist media to bash Republicans, weather *absolutely does* equal climate. Hurricanes Florence and Michael led to some awe-inspiring takes from non-scientists in the mainstream press:

"There's an old joke that a conservative is a liberal who's been mugged. Maybe it's time for an update: someone who believes in the climate crisis is a former climate denier whose community has been slammed by a hurricane," said Steve Benen, whose expertise lies in producing The Rachel Maddow Show.[17]

Benen had previously berated Trump for confusing climate with weather, saying "Now, at this point, we could talk about the fact that cold weather in a small part of the planet in late December does not disprove climate change."[18]

MSNBC has climate-grifting down to a science—pun intended. Not only do they make money by scaring the daylights out of people with terms like "climate crisis," and effortlessly blur the line between weather and climate when it is politically expedient, but they also pander to their base by bashing Trump at the same time.

In an article titled "Victims of Hurricane Michael are represented by climate deniers," John Abraham of *The Guardian* issued this grave message:

"Elections have consequences. Denying science has consequences. And we are reaping what we sow.... Good luck Florida and Georgia. My thoughts are with you. See you on the other side."

In other words, Trump and his electorate are responsible for Hurricane Michael and we're all gonna die.

In an article scoffing at Republicans as intellectual peons for not joining the Church of Climate Change after Hurricane Michael, *The New York Times*' Nicholas Kristof quoted M.I.T. "hurricane expert" Kerry Emanuel:

"There is strong consensus among scientists who study hurricanes and climate that warming temperatures should make more intense hurricanes possible," Emanuel said.[19]

How could anyone question the "strong consensus" that warming temperatures "should" make stronger hurricanes "possible?" With such a bulletproof consensus in place, the American taxpayer would be foolish not to immediately allocate trillions of hard-earned dollars for the vague promise of cutting carbon emissions, all while the world's largest polluters—India and China—do nothing. To their detriment, Americans would have the privilege of footing the bill, and also to their detriment they wouldn't even get a guarantee that the problem—which might not even be a problem—would be solved. What a deal!

That, of course, is what Barack Obama had planned upon entering the Paris Climate Accord. It was a massive transfer of wealth out of the pockets of Americans and into the hands of unelected, unaccountable, global bureaucrats under the pretext of a shoddy scientific "consensus."

Trump rightfully shredded the deal, for which the corporate media shredded him.

Robinson Meyer of *The Atlantic* bemoaned the fact that war-torn Syria had joined the Climate Accord, while the U.S. chose to sit it out.

"It's official. When it comes to climate change, there's now literally everyone else—and then there's the United States. Syria, the last remaining holdout from the Paris Agreement on climate change, announced at a United Nations meeting in Germany Tuesday that it will sign the agreement," Meyer said.[20]

It's settled, then! Syria is an objectively better country than America. Forget the ISIS beheadings. Pay no mind to the Syrians starving to death in the desert.[21] Never mind the mass-killing of Christians.[22] Their carbon emissions numbers look great! If only the moronic D.C. political journalists would all move to Syria, perhaps America could once again reign supreme.

Two years after rejecting the Paris Climate Accord, there is virtually zero evidence to show that the United States' withdrawal has allowed some unmitigated "climate crisis" to continue.[23]

Trump's rejection of massive spending on climate change initiatives was not his only agenda item that was supposed to end in our fiery deaths, according to our completely sane and rational news media. The introduction of the Tax Cuts and Jobs Act in late 2017, which subsequently passed through both chambers of Congress and was signed into law, was supposed to have cataclysmic consequences.

Former Clinton Treasury Department official Larry Summers claimed on CNBC's "Squawk Box" that tax cuts for corporations and the middle class would kill ten thousand people per year in the United States.[24]

"I think this bill is very dangerous," he said. "When people lose health insurance, they're less likely to get preventive care, they're more likely to defer health care they need, and ultimately they're more likely to die."

The bill included the repeal of the infamous Obamacare individual mandate, which forced Americans who did not have health insurance to purchase it from the government. The problem with the individual mandate, in sum, is that the federal government sucks at everything, especially providing healthcare. Look at the 300,000 veterans who died waiting for care at the hands of government-run Veterans Affairs hospitals for proof.[25]

Most of the Obamacare plans had massive deductibles. The actual insurance wouldn't kick in unless you fell off an amusement park ride or drove your bicycle off a cliff. But the monthly premiums for the insurance were relatively expensive. So, if you buckled up tight on the roller coaster and wore your helmet while cycling, chances are you'd end up footing a huge bill by the end of the year for insurance you didn't use. It boiled down to a useless, but very expensive tax.

All Trump did was tell Americans that they no longer had to purchase insurance from the feds if they did not want it. He did not say that Americans could not purchase insurance from the feds, if, say, they were brain dead—coincidentally the only condition for which Obamacare may have been useful.

But the media, excited to capitalize on the return of free market health insurance, spun Trump's tax cut into ten thousand deaths per year.

MSNBC's Joy Reid shamelessly politicized the harmless bill, too. Ultra-left author Bruce Bartlett made an appearance on Reid's show and made the totally reasonable claim that the tax bill was "akin to rape."[26] Reid made no attempt to tone down the hyperbole. The only rape that took place was the forceful coercion of Americans into purchasing government-subsidized healthcare in the first place, which was so awful that Bartlett's comments are insulting to rapists.

House Minority Leader Nancy Pelosi (D-CA) said that the tax bill was "the end of the world," for which she received generous media coverage.[27]

"The debate over health care is life and death," she continued. "This is Armageddon."

In the same press conference, she called the bill "the worst bill in the history of the United States Congress."

Say what you will about Pelosi, but she sure has a grasp on the type of manufactured outrage that drives the mainstream press. The worst three bills in history are obviously the Tax Cuts and Jobs Act of 2017, the Fugitive Slave Act of 1850, and the Indian Removal Act of 1830, in that order.

New York Times columnist Kurt Eichenwald mourned the loss of America as a whole after the tax bill was passed.

"America died tonight.... Millenials [sic]: move away if you can. USA is over. We killed it," he Tweeted.[28]

Though Eichenwald's directive is appealing (I wish millennials would move away too, and I say this as a millennial), I think he's clutching his pearls a bit too tightly. America survived a civil war, two world wars, a great depression, and Barack Obama's eight-year presidency. If anything will kill us, it won't be a few extra bucks in the pockets of the middle class.

When the press was not busy warning of our impending death from a Republican tax break, they were busy leveling with us, or at least doing the leftist equivalent of leveling. After the original freak-out, the messaging turned from "you're all gonna die," to "okay, you probably won't die, but this is still a bad bill because it was conceived by evil Republicans."

Washington Post columnist Catherine Rampell wrote a reasonably-titled column called "Apparently Republicans want to kick the middle class in the face."[29]

> *It's not enough to give money to rich people. Apparently, Republicans want to kick the poor and middle class in the face, too. I used to think the Republican Party's obsession with top-heavy tax cuts was about pleasing wealthy donors and maybe also fulfilling some misguided Randian fantasy. If the poor and middle class happened to be collateral damage, so be it. But it's starting to look like shafting the little guy has become a feature, not a bug, of the GOP's budget-busting tax plan.*

Charles Krauthammer, God rest his soul, once said that a fundamental rule of American politics is that conservatives think liberals are stupid, but liberals think conservatives are evil. Rampell's column is a case study in that fundamental rule. Instead of taking issue with the policy itself, she ascribes evil to the people who made the policy. For this reason, Republicans should avoid negotiating with Democrats. There is no such thing as "bipartisanship" when one side believes the other is subhuman.

Robert S. McElvaine, author of a rousing title called *F#*k You!—A Brief History of Sexism, from 'Prehistory' to Trump*, blasted the GOP's tax cuts, also in *The Washington Post*.

> *The GOP has been singing from the Market-is-God hymnal for well over a century, telling us that deregulation, tax cuts for the rich, and the concentration of ever more wealth in the bloated accounts of the richest people will result in prosperity for the rest of us. The party is now trying to pass a scam that throws a few crumbs to the middle class (temporarily—millions of middle-class Americans will soon see a tax hike if the bill is enacted) while heaping benefits on the super-rich, multiplying the national debt and endangering the American economy.*[30]

Pelosi scoffed at bonuses doled out by large companies en masse to their employees in the wake of the largest tax cut in modern history, too, calling them "crumbs."[31]

This is an apt time to describe a simple rule of thumb that the intelligentsia, in their haste to denounce anything Trump does as catastrophic, have either ignored or never bothered to consider. The top 1 percent of income earners in the United States pay roughly 90 percent of all federal income taxes.[32] Thus, when everyone gets a tax break, it is a mathematical truism that the top income earners—that is, the wealthiest people—will receive the largest tax cut in whole numbers. So, if one earns $1 million per year, and receives a 5 percent tax break, he saves $50,000. If one earns $100,000 per year and receives the *exact same* 5 percent tax break, he saves $5,000.

That is what liberals are constantly yakking about on cable news when they say Trump's tax cuts benefit only the wealthiest Americans and not the middle class. When the mass media says that Trump's tax cut is "for the wealthy," it is a political sleight-of-hand. *The tax cuts are only for the rich! Pay no attention to the man behind the curtain!*

In fact, Americans at large will save $1,400 in taxes in the 2018 fiscal year, according to the Heritage Foundation.[33] Middle class couples with two children will have saved an average of about $3,000. Hardly crumbs, as suggested by multi-millionaire Nancy Pelosi and the wealthy coast-dwelling elites at *The Washington Post.* And, for those who do not want their "crumbs," there is always the option of cutting a check to the federal government for the amount saved due to the tax cuts. Simply make it payable to the Internal Revenue Service, and mail it on over to Washington, D.C. The IRS will happily cash the check. I'm betting that none of the talking heads bemoaning tax cuts on cable news will choose that option.

For safe measure, *The New York Times*' Paul Krugman chimed in about the tax cuts for the middle class, arguing that they showed the "moral rot" within the Republican party. It is comforting to the ordinary American, I'm sure, to know that Krugman thinks they are rotten for not wanting to fork over all of their hard-earned cash to federal government.[34]

"First, it is not, at a fundamental level, a story about Donald Trump, bad as he is: the "rot" pervades the whole Republican Party. Second, the rot is wide as well as deep. I'm not just talking about Republican politicians, although the tax debate should dispel any remaining illusions about their motives. Just about every G.O.P. member of Congress, including the sainted late John McCain, is willing to put partisan loyalty above principle, voting for what they have to know is terrible and irresponsible legislation," Krugman wrote.

Economists appear to be foggy on whether tax cuts correlate to economic growth, and they are certainly not giving Trump the benefit of the doubt. But nearly one year after Trump's massive tax cut for everyone, consumer confidence has hit a seventeen-year high,[35] GDP has continued to grow, unemployment has continued to drop, and the stock market is roaring. It certainly appears to the naked eye as though the naysayers and doomsday conspiracy theorists in the mainstream press were wrong, a position with which they are familiar. As an added bonus, not one person has died from tax cuts!

If you've made it this far into this book, then you have also not died in one of the many fiery nuclear wars that the press predicted Trump would start. World Wars III, IV, and V with Iran, Russia and North Korea, respectively, should have at least commenced if not finished by now; judging by the mainstream media's fervor in reporting the dangers of Trump having possession of the nuclear launch codes. The media said Trump was too reckless to possess such powers, as though he would write the codes on the back of his golf scorecard just in case he needed to launch a mid-round nuke from the turn at Mar-a-Lago.

Trump must have repeated the slogan "Peace Through Strength" thousands of times on the campaign trail, relentlessly bashing Hillary Clinton for her participation in the destruction of the Middle East, and for her apparent willingness to continue down that disastrous path. Trump's message was that America does not have to resort to violence. All we have to do is make sure the rest of the world knows that we have the largest *huevos* on the block. You might recall Trump denouncing the Iraq war during his campaign, and vowing to bring American troops home from Afghanistan and Syria.[36] Ordinary people both understood and loved the "peace through strength" message. They knew that Trump wouldn't travel the world kissing rings of foreign dignitaries like his predecessor and, more importantly, they were *tired* of endless wars. He would make it known to the world that America does not want a fight, but that if one broke out there would be hell to pay.

The press did not understand that message as well as ordinary Americans, never having taken the time to get to know them. (Author's note: I met CNN's Brian Stelter at a Trump rally in Charlotte, North Carolina in October 2018. He told me that it was the first Trump rally he had ever attended, and that his biggest regret of the 2016 campaign cycle was never having attended a rally during the Trump campaign. Stelter hosts a show called "Reliable Sources." Apparently, he is not the reliable source.)

Indeed, the press was completely flummoxed by Trump's messaging. On one hand, Trump was professing peace. On the other hand, they needed to sell advertisements. So, they conjured up the narrative that regardless of whether Trump was well-intentioned, and regardless of whether or not he actually wanted peace, he was too hot-headed and reckless to command the world's strongest military, and that he lacked a coherent foreign policy strategy.

The following *Washington Post* headline from April 2018 sums this narrative up perfectly: "Trump may not intend to start a war. But he sure could bumble into one,"[37] by the *Post's* Deputy Editorial Page Editor Jackson Diehl.

> *The main danger, then, is not that Trump will choose war. It is that he will stumble into it, through impulsive acts unattached to any coherent strategy. He has set up two big, high-risk decision points for this spring: on whether to renew sanctions on Iran in mid-May and whether to deal with North Korea's Kim Jong Un at a summit by the end of that month. If he accepts a face-saving bargain on Iran with the Europeans, or a promise by Kim to denuclearize, he will contradict everything that the notoriously inflexible Bolton has stood for over decades—raising the question of why Trump hired him.*

Trump tore up the Iran nuclear deal and hit them with new sanctions, and told North Korea to stop building nukes if they ever wanted to trade again with China, upon whose coal and oil they rely to exist.[38] No one has heard a peep from Iran in months, and Kim Jong-un has committed to fully denuclearizing, returned the remains of American soldiers killed in the Korean War, and freed three American hostages. Oh yeah, and we're all still alive!

Still, in June 2018, the press was pegging Trump as a dunce with his finger on the nuclear button. This time, the media claimed that Russia would do us in.

Express, a British mainstream press publication, quoted American director of the James Martin Center for Nonproliferation Studies in California, Dr. William Potter, as saying the following: "But based on his actions to date, there is little to suggest that Mr Trump has any conception of the risks of nuclear war, the dangers of nuclear weapons spread, or how US-Russian cooperation can be employed to mitigate these threats."[39]

This assessment from a random academic in California, cited by the mainstream press in their continued effort to spread fear and terrorize the masses, is completely devoid of any logic or reasoning, and certainly cannot be explained "based on Trump's actions."

Trump averted an impending crisis with North Korea, with whom America was on a warpath during the Obama years, and forced the Hermit Kingdom into a complete 180 from aggressive attack dog to lazy front-porch hound. Still, somehow Potter deduced that Trump has no "conception of the risks of nuclear war." And the media gladly wrote a headline based on that not-so-brilliant analysis.

Jeffrey Lewis of *Wired* warned that Trump would start a nuclear war via Twitter.[40]

"'Twitter could get us into a war,'" Lewis quoted. "That sentence, which appears in Bob Woodward's new book, *Fear*, about the Trump Administration, has shocked a lot of people.

Not me. Because I just wrote a novel in which precisely that same thing happens. And let me tell you: It's not far-fetched."

Lewis wrote another apocalyptic piece in *The Independent*. It was front-to-back speculation about our certain death, titled "This is how nuclear war with North Korea would unfold, step by step,"[41] which can best be described as Armageddon fan-fiction. The article predicts:

March 2019: *This time, the North Koreans went too far.*

...When a South Korean airliner crossed over into North Korean airspace, a Northern air defence crew, already jumpy and anticipating the allied maneouvres [sic] in the Sea of Japan, mistook it for an American bomber. The crew fired a surface-to-air missile, sending the plane plunging into the ocean, killing all 250 people on board.

The South Korean public was outraged. Within hours, Moon ordered South Korean missile units to strike the air defence battery, as well as select leadership targets throughout North Korea. Moon's limited missile strike might have been enough by itself to start the nuclear war of 2019. South Korean and American officials are still trading accusations. But the surviving members of the Moon administration insist that things would have been fine had President Donald Trump not picked up his smartphone: "LITTLE ROCKET MAN WON'T BE AROUND MUCH LONGER!"

Scarier than the prospect of nuclear war is that some people actually take this garbage seriously. Real reporters and serious publications do not salivate over the prospect of nuclear war, creating a fake narrative, and casting the leader of the free world as a villain. Then again, with all the hyperbole and false predictions, the mainstream press isn't really taken seriously these days.

CHAPTER 3

WHITE HATE

The mainstream press has made it abundantly clear that the only acceptable form of racism in America in 2018 is racism against white people, specifically white men.

Ann Coulter wrote a fabulous column called "No More Mr. White Guy,"[42] in which she chronicled the anti-white racism directed at the Senate Judiciary Committee during the Brett Kavanaugh hearings before they questioned Christine Blasey Ford. Here is a sampling of quotes from the column:

> *"They know the optics of 11 white men questioning Dr. Ford...will be so harmful and so damaging to the GOP."*—*Areva Martin, CNN legal analyst*

> *"They understand that you have all of these white men who would be questioning this woman...the optics of it would look terrible."*—*Gloria Borger, CNN chief political analyst*

> *"What are those—that collection of old white men going to do?"*—*Cynthia Alksne, MSNBC contributor*

"Once again, it will be all white men on the Republican side of the Judiciary Committee."—CNN anchor Poppy Harlow

"What hasn't changed is the number of white men questioning, certainly, on the Republican side."—Dana Bash, CNN chief political correspondent

The evil white men on the Senate Judiciary Committee clearly received the mainstream press's message loud and clear. They declined to question Ford themselves, instead hiring Rachel Mitchell, an experienced sex crimes prosecutor from Maricopa County, Arizona to handle the inquiry. In any case, *so what* if they had questioned Ford? These "11 white men" were duly elected Senators. It was their job to question Ford, regardless of their race.

Democrats had a crowd of Senators on the Committee who were present to question Ford, too, and some of them expressed their disdain for the white man as well.

Senator "Crazy" Mazie Hirono (D-HI) is a Japanese-American Congresswoman. She is a member of the esteemed Judiciary Committee who told men to "do the right thing for a change" and "shut up" in the face of the allegations against Kavanaugh.[43] Due to her gender and nationality, the mainstream press let those demonstrably misandrist comments slide. In fact, she was applauded by the third-wave feminist crowd. *Roll Call*'s Patricia Murphy fawned over her in an opinion piece, calling her a "badass."[44]

Hirono lit the internet on fire last week when she said men in America need to 'shut up and step up' on sexual assault allegations like the ones Kavanaugh now faces from multiple accusers.... She was meme'd, loved, and completely lionized for having the Hawaiian coconuts to speak her mind as a member of the Senate Judiciary Committee tasked with vetting Kavanaugh's nomination as it twisted and turned toward its messy possible conclusion this week.

Make no mistake, Hirono was not speaking to all men when she told them to "shut up." She was speaking to white men. Had her rhetoric been directed towards black men, it would have been a bridge too far, even for the scumbags in the mainstream press. But for white men, her sexism and misandry were just right.

Senator Lindsey Graham (R-SC) knew exactly who Hirono was barking at, and he clarified her comments for the rest of America during a nationally televised committee meeting days after Hirono's outburst.

"I know I'm a single white male from South Carolina, and I'm told I should shut up, but I will not shut up, if that's okay," he said while staring Hirono down.[45]

Kavanaugh himself was the target of anti-white hatred during the proceedings, too.

The Washington Post published a column called "Hell Hath No Fury Like an Entitled White Man Denied," written by MSNBC Contributor Jonathan Capehart.[46] He was responding to Kavanaugh's justifiable indignation over the unprovable accusations of sexual misconduct made by Democrats as a political stunt that permanently tarnished his reputation. Reading the headline alone, one might think that race-baiting Capehart had simply forgotten that black Supreme Court Justice Clarence Thomas was outraged in his own response to Anita Hill's accusations of sexual harassment during Thomas's 1991 confirmation hearings. But Capehart did not forget. Instead, he chose to be downright malicious and openly racist. He managed to reconcile Thomas's anger as justified, but Kavanaugh's as "entitlement" simply because Thomas is black, and Kavanaugh is white.

Capehart even shamelessly copped to his own hypocrisy.

He called Kavanaugh's "display of white (male) entitlement especially galling" and bashed him for his "lack of humility and decorum and contrition." Then, after admitting that Kavanaugh's opening resembled Thomas's, Capehart explained that he had empathy for Thomas because Thomas was black.

"Back then, I couldn't help but feel a pang of empathy for Thomas," he said. "As an African American, I understood Thomas's controlled fury."

This is textbook racism. But the liberal media repeatedly gets away with it.

Associate editor of the *Sacramento Bee*, Erika D. Smith, wrote a similar column in that publication called "A Crying Brett Kavanaugh. This is What White Male Privilege Looks Like."[47] She, too, was unhappy with Kavanaugh's whiteness and his response to the allegations against him.

"To the loyal, populist supporters of President Donald Trump, Kavanaugh succeeded in looking like a victim of elitist politicians," she wrote. "But to the rest of us, he just looked like an entitled, privileged white male, whining because he's unaccustomed to losing anything—much less a lifetime appointment to the nation's highest court that he always expected to get."

How dare Kavanaugh have the gall to attempt to clear his good name *and* be white. In progressive America, white men are no longer allowed to express the emotion of anger. They cannot possibly be genuinely angry—only upset that their "privilege" is being called into question. This is the attitude of the mainstream press.

Bitterness towards white men spewed from the mouths of sniveling social justice snots and bitter, single, third-wave feminists is a common practice in the mainstream press. White men are universally hated by the media, even by other white men. White men in media have even learned to hate themselves so they will continue to be invited to fancy cocktail parties with their elitist "progressive" friends. They aren't even trying to hide it. All it takes is a quick glance at Twitter archives to find out just what white mainstream press writers and newsies think about other white people.

Self-loathing Matthew Dowd, ABC's Chief Political Analyst, wrote a column in October 2018 called "Us White Male Christians Need to Step Back and Give Others Room to Lead."[48] He argued:

Instead of waiting for the diverse population of America to keep pushing and prodding, I would humbly suggest that we as white male Christians take it upon ourselves to step back and give more people who don't look like us

> *access to the levers of power. Yes, let me repeat, we as*
> *white male Christians should do what real leadership*
> *demands and practice a level of humility which demon-*
> *strates strength by stepping back from the center of the*
> *room and begin to give up our seats at the table.*

Dowd pitched this utterly ridiculous idea as the morally just course of action. Leftists and their media ilk, responsible for everything from the sexual revolution to the abortion pill—and the steady decline of American morality in between—ought not to be lecturing the rest of us on morality. Then again, self-awareness is not their strength either.

Dowd was on the receiving end of a massive amount of flack for his opinion piece, and was buried in a chorus of "you first" Tweets in response its publication. While advising ordinary white Christian males to give up their positions of "power," Dowd is unwilling to give up his cushy gig, which he uses in attempts to sway the opinion of an entire nation. Dowd has more power than almost every other white male in America. Maybe one day he'll put his money where his mouth is.

Speaking of Twitter, it is a treasure trove of anti-white hatred from white people in media. Here are a few samplings:

> *"I HATE WHITE PEOPLE," Tweeted* Esquire *contrib-*
> *utor and white man Pete Forester in 2018.*[49]

> *"Yeah. White people are stupid," Tweeted former*
> *conservative and current writer at* Daily Beast *and* The
> Atlantic, *Ben Howe. Howe, who Tweeted this in response*
> *to Geraldo Rivera, is also white.*[50]

Catherine Deveny is a white comedienne and newspaper columnist from Australia who said on Twitter that "white people suck."[51]

"Fuck white people," said Christina Warren, a white former journalist of Gizmodo and Mashable on Twitter. I use the word "journalist" loosely in this context.[52]

"We need white genocide more than ever," Tweeted white HuffPost *columnist Dan Arel.[53]*

There are hundreds more examples of comments like these from mainstream press writers archived online.

But white people in the press are not alone in hating the entire white population of America. In August 2018, *The New York Times* hired Sarah Jeong as a member of its formerly prestigious editorial board. Within hours, internet sleuths dug up a host of anti-white comments that she had made on Twitter over the years.[54] She Tweeted:

"Dumbass fucking white people marking up the internet with their opinions like dogs pissing on fire hydrants."

"1) white men are bullshit 2) no one cares about women 3) you can threaten anyone on the internet except cops"

"White people have stopped breeding. You'll all go extinct soon. This was my plan all along."

> *"Are white people genetically predisposed to burn faster in the sun, thus logically being only fit to live underground like groveling goblins."*

Naturally, the *Times* faced backlash over Jeong's long history of white hate. So, they responded by doing what any normal press organization would do when caught hiring a racist editor: they blamed racism.

"[Jeong's] journalism and the fact that she is a young Asian woman have made her a subject of frequent online harassment," the *Times* wrote in a statement. "For a period of time, she responded to that harassment by imitating the rhetoric of harassers."[55]

See, Jeong was not being racist herself, she was just imitating racists. That explains it! For the record, though, she did a fantastic job playing the role of a racist. But for the assurance from the *Times* that she was only joking, I would have totally pegged her as hater of the entire white race. Thankfully, the paper cleared that up with their statement.

The *Times'* bogus excuse raises a valid question: In what other arenas does the "imitation" defense apply? "I'm sorry, officer, I'm not actually an axe murderer. I was just imitating an axe murderer! I'll be on my way now. By the way, do you know where can I find a copy of today's *New York Times*?"

Despite the calls for white genocide from the likes of Sarah Jeong, according to the mainstream press, white genocide is just a "conspiracy theory," and anyone who mentions it is guilty of echoing "white supremacist" talking points.

That was exactly what happened to Tucker Carlson when he mentioned white genocide in the context of an appalling Tweet by Georgetown professor Christine Fair.

"Look at thus [sic] chorus of entitled white men justifying a serial rapist's arrogated entitlement. All of them deserve miserable deaths while feminists laugh as they take their last gasps. Bonus: we castrate their corpses and feed them to swine? Yes."[56]

Fair Tweeted that very reasonable message in response to an impassioned speech given by Lindsey Graham, in which he denounced Democrats who so lust for power that during the Kavanaugh confirmation hearings they ruined the innocent man's life.

But when Carlson mentioned in passing on his show that Fair was calling for white genocide, he was relentlessly crushed by the mainstream press.

"Tucker Carlson's Racist Dog Whistle of the Night is White 'Genocide'," said a headline by Splinter's Jack Crosbie.[57]

"Tucker Carlson is no stranger to white nationalist talking points, and tonight he didn't disappoint. The Fox anchor hosts America's third-largest cable news show, and on Monday night he used that platform to alert his audiences to the dangers of liberals who support white genocide," Crosbie wrote in defense of the professor.

Calling for the gruesome deaths of all white men? Fine by the mainstream press! Mention that maybe the left's rhetoric is borderline genocidal? You're a white nationalist conspiracy theorist! These are the rules as currently dictated by the left-wing media.

The same left-wing media often employs another slippery tactic to avoid discussing their obvious disdain for white people. In order to justify hiring demonstrably anti-white racists, they'll often write columns denying that anti-white racism exists.

Vice did just that in October 2016. The column was titled "Dear White People, Please Stop Pretending Reverse Racism is Real."[58] The column, written by Manisha Krishnan, was sub-headlined "It's literally impossible to be racist to a white person." Krishnan is a "Senior Writer" at *Vice*, a position apparently reserved for the most virulently racist among the bunch.

For her piece, Krishnan interviewed a Toronto human rights lawyer named Anthony Morgan, whom she presented as an expert on the subject of racism—perhaps not something he'd want written on his tombstone, lest it be taken out of context. She framed the piece in the context of Black Lives Matter, and attempted to debunk the idea that the group is a violent, radical separatist movement for black supremacists who riot (see Ferguson, Missouri) and loot (see Charlotte, North Carolina) in lieu of peaceful protest and honest conversation.

"'When you're so deeply invested in your privilege, and in this case white privilege, racial equality feels like oppression,'" Krishnan quoted Morgan. She continued, "Simply put, Morgan said reverse racism doesn't exist and a person who claims otherwise is 'outing themselves as someone who has little to no experience or knowledge of what racism is.'"

Forgive me for questioning the sacrosanct wisdom and expertise of a random lawyer from Toronto, but what in God's name is this clown talking about? It has been made very clear by social justice wonks in media like Sarah Jeong that white genocide—the death of an entire race—is the explicit goal. But Morgan shrugs off those minor details, and then *Vice* publishes the piece. All of a sudden, it is frowned upon by the mainstream press for us simpletons to discourage the elimination of white people. How ghastly of us!

The Merriam Webster definition of racism is "a belief that race is the primary determinant of human traits and capacities and that racial differences produce an inherent superiority of a particular race." Any other definition is simply made up in an attempt at race-baiting by overeducated losers like Morgan and the staff at *Vice* who want to join the local social justice club because permanent outrage is currently in style. Morgan is right in one respect, though. Reverse racism does not exist. Anti-white racism is simply racism, like any other kind.

Somehow, media outlets publish stories advocating for the death of all white people and then miraculously claim that it is out of bounds for Trump to call them the enemy of the American people, even though America is a majority white nation.

The New York Times made no attempt at mincing words when it published an opinion piece by George Yancy called "Dear White America" in 2015.[59] To Yancy, all white people of all political persuasions are racists, and there is nothing they can do about it:

> If you are white, and you are reading this letter, I ask
> that you don't run to seek shelter from your own racism.
> Don't hide from your responsibility. Rather, begin, right
> now, to practice being vulnerable. Being neither a
> "good" white person nor a liberal white person will get

you off the proverbial hook.... Take another deep breath. I ask that you try to be "un-sutured." If that term brings to mind a state of pain, open flesh, it is meant to do so. After all, it is painful to let go of your "white innocence," to use this letter as a mirror, one that refuses to show you what you want to see, one that demands that you look at the lies that you tell yourself so that you don't feel the weight of responsibility for those who live under the yoke of whiteness, your whiteness.

Why bother attempting to reason with the leftist media elite? They will undoubtedly call all white people racist no matter what those white people say or do, and then call for their deaths. They will never be satisfied. They hate you and they want you dead. Attempting to appease them is akin to negotiating with terrorists. It shouldn't be attempted because they'll simply take more hostages. So, fuck them. If the social justice goal line is going to continuously be moved forward so that it is perpetually unreachable, why try to please them at all?

That is exactly how Trump approached his 2016 presidential run, and consequently how he won the presidency. He refused to cower to the mainstream press when they made bogus allegations of racism against him. He either shrugged it off and kept going, or skillfully doubled down. The media had never seen anything like it. They were used to weaklings like Jeb!, who told us approximately one million times that he spoke Spanish at home, in an attempt to prove how totally non-racist he was. What Jeb! and every other Republican candidate failed to understand—except for Trump—is that the media did not care how "tolerant" or "accepting" they tried to appear. The case was already closed. The leftists on cable news, like Yancy in his *New York Times* column, had already decided that they were racists for the simple fact that their skin was white, and there was nothing they could do about it. Attempting to pass these bad faith tests of anti-racism are a waste of time and political capital.

Instead of taking the low-T route, Trump flipped them a throbbing middle finger and pressed forward. And wouldn't you know, it worked? It turns out Americans wanted a candidate who would push back against the bullies in the press. Who could have imagined?

Trump blew the media goofballs off every time they falsely maligned him as a racist. Calling Trump a racist was like giving a parking ticket to a death row inmate. It meant nothing to him.

While consistently employing and publishing racists, the media breathlessly tossed around allegations of racism against Trump at every turn despite the tactic's lack of effectiveness against Trump, who made himself immune to such attacks.

HuffPost wrote a column in 2016 called "Here Are 13 Examples Of Donald Trump Being a Racist."[60] One of their primary beefs with Trump was that he refused to denounce former KKK leader David Duke, who they said was "campaigning for him." That was a lie. Duke never hit the Trump campaign trail. He might have voted for Trump, though that is not even certain. In any case, it wasn't like Duke was working for the Trump campaign. Nuance matters not to the left-wing media when they have a Republican to destroy.

Duke is politically impotent, and the KKK has fewer than three thousand members nationwide in a country with a population of 330 million.[61] Nobody supports Duke. If there ever was an example of fringe extremism, Duke is it. But he is like a show pony for the political left. Every four years, when Duke inevitably supports the Republican candidate, the mainstream press trots him out to show America how racist Republicans are. Pretending that Duke's racism is an accurate representation of Republicans' views on race is like claiming that Harvey Weinstein's rapes are an accurate representation of Democrats' views on sex. Harvey votes Democrat! They must all be rapists!

If not for the attention that Duke receives during every election cycle from the likes of CNN, who interviewed Trump in an attempt to bully him into disavowing the Klan leader, the KKK would have sunken into obscurity by now, never to be heard from again. The press cannot let that happen, though. In their minds, Duke is an instrumental part of the playbook for hurting Republicans.

Trump claimed that he did not know who Duke was during the interview with Jake Tapper. CNN and *HuffPost* apparently didn't buy that story, because they truly believe that Duke's beliefs are in line with the entirety of the political right, which is simply untrue. But if the press took to the streets to ask ordinary Americans to identify David Duke, they would receive only blank stares. This is a country in which 61 percent of the population does not even know the words to "The Star-Spangled Banner."[62] Only 26 percent of Americans can name the three branches of government.[63] Ordinary people have no clue who David Duke is, and given the chance would denounce his extremism. That is precisely why Trump's failure to denounce Duke meant absolutely nothing to anyone outside of the Beltway journo club. Still, the media tried to equate every Republican, Trump included, with Duke and the KKK.

Coincidentally, *HuffPost* never asked Hillary Clinton about her connection to Robert Byrd, a former KKK Grand Wizard whom she called "her mentor." I'm sure that was simply an innocent omission.

In the same piece, *HuffPost* called Trump a racist for "treating racial groups like monoliths." Here is an example they provided:

"I'll take jobs back from China, I'll take jobs back from Japan," Trump said during his visit to the U.S.-Mexican border in July. "The Hispanics are going to get those jobs, and they're going to love Trump."

Trump: I'm going to create jobs for Hispanic people.

HuffPost: But that's racist!

How could that possibly be construed as racist? Trump was talking about his plan to help Hispanic-Americans get jobs—which, last I checked, is a critical element to avoiding poverty and misery—and *HuffPost* called him a racist for it.

Unsatisfied, the publication wrote another piece only months later called "Here Are 16 Examples of Donald Trump Being Racist."[64] This article was apparently written for those *HuffPost* readers who suffer from short-term memory loss, as many of the examples were duplicates from the previous article.

One of the examples in the second anti-Trump hit piece was the president's executive order temporarily halting travel from several Muslim-majority nations. This, *HuffPost* reported, was a "Muslim ban" from the United States (there's that lack of nuance again).

But Trump never explicitly banned Muslims from traveling to the United States. Nationality, not religion, was the central element of the ban. Indeed, Christians in Syria, just like their Muslim counterparts, are temporarily blocked from entering this country. It was for precisely this reason that the Supreme Court upheld the ban, certifying that it was within Trump's purview as Commander in Chief, and totally Constitutional.[65]

As usual, *HuffPost* didn't let the facts get in the way of the "racist Trump" narrative. The piece said:

> *A blanket ban on travel from those countries and anti-Muslim bigotry in general is "essentially an extension of the fear and vilification of not only Muslims but everyone perceived to be Muslim that's been taking place for centuries," Khaled Beydoun, a law professor at the University of Detroit who also works with the Islamophobia Research and Documentation Project at the University of California, Berkeley, explained.*

Without providing any examples other than the non-racist "Muslim ban," *HuffPost* reasoned that Trump was a racist because of "bigotry in general." Well, I think that *HuffPost* is an idiotic publication, and I'm citing their "idiocy in general" to prove my point. That settles that!

The press has a well-documented history of calling every Republican candidate for public office in the past half-century a racist. Listening to the press discuss Republican presidential candidates, one would have to conclude that either Republicans are the dumbest people on earth for continuously running racist candidates or that the press is lying. In this case, like most others, the press is lying.

Associated Press reporter Robert Parry managed to make Mitt Romney, perhaps the most boring candidate ever to run for the presidency, into a racist during Romney's 2012 bid. Romney once quipped that no one had ever asked to see his birth certificate, taking a swipe at Barack Obama over the confusion surrounding Obama's place of birth. Parry near soiled himself over this tiny slight.

"Romney may not be a crude racist, the sort who would dress up in white sheets and burn crosses on someone's lawn," he said in a column. "But America has had a long and equally grim history of country-club racists whose personal contempt toward blacks, Hispanics, Arabs and other dark-skinned people is cloaked in more genteel phrasing."[66]

Alas, John McCain was a racist, too, when he ran for president in 2008.

In an article called "Palling around with racists,"[67] *The Guardian*'s Lola Adesioye argued that both McCain and his running mate Sarah Palin were "asking their supporters if a black man should be president":

> It can be argued that much of the Republicans' recent rhetoric carries a racial subtext and that, unable to openly use Obama's race as weapon, they instead employ coded language which is [sic] suggests that

Obama is different, foreign and 'other.' Sarah Palin, for example, says "[Obama] is not a man who sees America the way you and I see America." There is no doubt that the 'you and I' she is referring to are white Americans: the Joe Six Packs and the hockey moms that she constantly talks about.

But then, nearly a decade later, something amazing happened. When McCain defied Trump from his deathbed, he became a national hero in the media. After he died of brain cancer, the same leftist press that bashed him as a racist lavished him with praise. It was a truly unbelievable spectacle. They simply expected us to forget what they had said a mere ten years earlier and trust that, this time around, they were being honest in their characterizations of McCain. What a sham!

"Over many years I saw McCain repeatedly speak up on issues where there was zero political return," said Nicholas Kristof in *The New York Times*. "Whether it was human trafficking victims (also a great cause of Cindy McCain), Syrians being bombed, Rohingya facing genocide or terrorism suspects facing torture, McCain did not follow voters but tried to lead them; he tried to do the right thing."[68]

There was not one mention of John McCain's alleged racism post-2008.

The press pulled the same gag when President George H. W. Bush died, pretending that he was an extraordinary statesman whom they greatly admired, though they relentlessly bashed him throughout his presidency. Right-wing *Townhall* columnist Kurt Schlichter wrote a brilliant column about this mainstream press paradox called "The Only Good Republican is a Dead Republican,"[69] wherein he detailed the liberal admiration for Republicans—after their deaths.

Between hiring racists, covering for racists when it is politically expedient, and calling Republicans racists at every turn, the press has committed racism seppuku. Worse, it has killed the meaning of the word. If everything is racist, then nothing is racist. If a real racist ever comes along, we will be in real danger. The overuse of the term has led ordinary Americans to roll their eyes whenever the alarmist press uses it.

In charging forward regardless of what they called him, Trump signaled to the American people that they did not have to buy into the "racism" narrative either. He fought for them, and gave them the confidence to express their own political beliefs without fear of reprisal. Instead of rolling over and begging for mercy like candidates before him, he grappled with the enemy in the streets. And he won. It was a valuable lesson in dealing with the biased, hate-filled left-wing media. Taking the offensive against them is a much wiser tactic than attempting to play by their rules and begging for mercy that will never be granted.

CHAPTER 4

THE "EXPERTS"

With so many "expert" pundits in the media constantly screwing up predictions and analysis on every subject, it's a wonder that America can't find any dunces to replace them. Name the item, and the press has been wrong about it.

When weathermen get the forecast wrong, which happens often, we laugh it off because the weather is notoriously difficult to predict, and mostly inconsequential. But somehow, the commentariat, which has a far worse record than the poor saps in the weather business, yet far more responsibility to the American public, consistently gets a pass for its misdeeds.

The most obvious example was the mainstream press's horrible work predicting the 2016 election results. There was not a single notable press outlet that predicted that President Trump would win on November 8, 2016. The press even worked actively against Trump, spending months willing Hillary Clinton to victory by telling American voters time after time that Trump didn't have a chance. They were wrong.

"Newsflash: It's Going to Be Hillary Vs. Jeb," *Politico* headlined a not-so-prescient story by Bill Scher in May 2015.[70]

"You can turn off Fox, MSNBC, and CNN; you can close Twitter; you can sign off your crazy uncle's Facebook feed," Scher said. "I am going to tell you, right now, what the political landscape of the future looks like so you don't waste your time over the next year listening to a parade of pundits or watching those ridiculous primary debates. The 2016 election is going to come down to Hillary vs. Jeb, of course. Dynasty against dynasty."

Low energy Jeb! didn't even make it to the final Republican primary debate. In fact, he dropped out of the race after the fourth-to-last primary debate, a February 13, 2016 Trump trouncing in Greenville, South Carolina.

Scher would have been wrong about Clinton, too, had the DNC not rigged the Democratic primary in her favor, gypping Bernie Sanders.

Karen Tumulty and Matea Gold of *The Washington Post* went all-in on Jeb! even earlier, in January 2015.[71]

"Republicans have a tradition of picking an anointed one early," they explained. "That establishment candidate almost always ends up with the nomination."

On the subject of those primary races, *FiveThirtyEight* predicted with 99 percent certainty that Clinton would beat Sanders in the Michigan Democratic primary. Sanders ended up winning Michigan by 1.5 percent of the vote. The poor polling breathlessly parroted by the hollow men in media would later be described by *FiveThirtyEight*'s Nate Silver, a poll analyst often cited by mainstream press pundits, as "among the worst polling errors in primary history."[72] (Wait till you see how the pollsters and press did in the general!) Of course, Clinton's loss in Michigan didn't matter. Due to the aforementioned rigging, Clinton still won eighty-one of the state's 147 delegates at the Democratic National Convention.[73] Sanders received sixty-six delegates and a case of chocolate pudding as a consolation prize.

Then there was conservatives' old pal, #NeverTrump nuisance Bill "Cruise Ship" Kristol, editor-at-large of *Weekly Standard*, a publication which, by the time this book is published, will have been mercifully put out of its misery like Old Yeller. Kristol is one of the last of a dying breed of cocktail conservatives who failed to conserve anything during his thirty years of public influence. In other words, he is exactly what Trump voters rejected when they took a pass on Jeb! and company and rallied behind Trump. Kristol hilariously predicted that there would be a viable independent candidate (a certain contradiction in terms) who would take the nation by storm during the general.

"There will be an independent candidate—an impressive one, with a strong team and a real chance," Kristol Tweeted in May 2016.[74]

That alleged candidate was David French of the *National Review*'s opinion section, another #NeverTrump "Republican." The only problem was that French had no idea he was running. He respectfully declined Kristol's nomination. Eventually, Kristol gave up on the awful predictions and vowed to vote for Clinton.[75] He is still a bitter Trump-hater to this day.

Former MSNBC host Keith Olbermann was spectacularly wrong about Trump, too.

"Because of the premise of the campaign, I don't think he has a reasonable chance of being elected. At this point, from what I'm hearing, I don't even think he's going to get the nomination. Because I think the Republican Party is going to say, everybody who is in the Republican Party goes if he wins, we all lose our jobs," he said on ABC's "The View" in March 2016.[76]

Clearly, "From what I'm hearing" is mainstream press speak for "I'm making this up on the fly." The whole reason Trump was elected was because of the "premise of the campaign," namely fewer illegals and more jobs. While the hosts of "The View" are liberal, ABC brought Olbermann on for diversity of opinion. He is a radical far leftist. After predicting that Trump would be more dangerous handling nuclear weapons than ISIS, he characterized the American people thusly:

"To be fair, who are the people who are supporting [Trump], generally speaking? What I'm saying is they're mostly people who can't really be trusted to find their own homes again once they leave them," he said.

Olbermann—generally speaking—is a condescending asshole. It turned out that all those Americans who have trouble "finding their homes again once they leave them" managed to get to and from the polls on election day without issue. After that, Olbermann was relegated to a political podcast on *GQ* that nobody watched. Then he threw a tantrum and quit politics for good, heading back over to ESPN, where he started his television career, for a less stressful gig.[77]

Right-wing firebrand Ann Coulter was nearly laughed off stage by a panel of political "experts" on "Real Time with Bill Maher" in June 2015 when she predicted that Donald Trump had the best chance of any declared Republican candidate to win the presidency.[78] The panel included MSNBC host

Joy-Ann Reid, *Daily Beast* columnist and frequent CNN guest Matt Lewis, and Rep. Luis Gutiérrez (D-IL.). The panel proved itself to be no more politically savvy than the audience, which also howled with laughter. Coulter would eventually have the last laugh.

The general election did not treat the "experts" any better than the primary.

On November 8, 2016, *FiveThirtyEight's* Nate Silver, after aggregated poll analysis, gave Trump a 28.6 percent chance of winning.[79] He predicted that Clinton would win swing states North Carolina, Pennsylvania, and Florida, along with generally-blue Wisconsin and Michigan. Trump won all five.

HuffPost famously predicted with 98 percent certainty that Clinton would take the White House,[80] clarifying that they ran ten million simulations based on their "state-by-state averages" and that Clinton won at least 270 electoral votes in 9.8 million of the simulations. If you're keeping score at home, that means that the publication was wrong 9.8 million times. It predicted that Trump would win only 215 electoral votes. He won 306.

Newsweek famously pre-printed a special edition of its magazine with the cover title "Madam President," commemorating what it thought would be Clinton's historic win. As of this writing, original recalled copies are selling for hundreds of dollars on eBay as novelty items.[81]

Stephen Colbert, a political operative and pundit disguised as a late-night comedian (a horrible disguise, at that), assured all of his leftist viewers that Trump would never be president.

"And so, Mr. Trump, right now, to answer your call for political honesty, I just wanna say, you're not gonna be president, all right?" Colbert said on his CBS show. "It's been fun. It's been great. I love you! But come on. Come on, buddy! All—let's say—cow poo poo aside, there is zero chance we'll be seeing you being sworn in on the Capitol steps with your hand on a giant golden bible."[82]

CNN was no more correct than the funny guy at CBS.

"Let's be clear: Donald Trump will lose the election," said CNN's Fareed Zakaria on his show just days before the final presidential debate.[83]

On the same network, political analyst Bob Beckel made the same prediction, which of course ended with the same outcome:

> *"Could I just cut through? I have one thing to say and one thing only, and that is that this race is over. Tomorrow morning, the money will dry up, the Republicans will start to hide, Trump has no place to go, this race, effectively, as of tonight is no longer a presidential race. Everything I know about presidential politics—and I've been through five of 'em—I've never seen one like this. This race is over. You might as well accept it. And the question now is 'how do you minimize damage.'"[84]*

All that expertise and experience, and Beckel ended up being the one hiding post-election. In fact, there should probably be a BOLO out for Beckel? Nobody has heard from him since that segment.

On the eve of the election, CNN political contributor Hilary Rosen was positive that Clinton would become the president-elect.

"It'll be interesting tomorrow night, I think, when Hillary Clinton wins, that Donald Trump will have lost this election from the very first day he announced," she said.[85]

For the critics who did not completely write off a Trump presidency, there were still plenty of awful takes to go around, particularly in the way of the American economy and stock market under Trump.

On September 26, 2016, *New York Times* journalist Kurt Eichenwald made the objectively worst pre-election prediction in American history.

"In preparation for a completely unpredictable Trump presidency, I sold all stocks in my kids' education accounts today. I urge u to do same," he said on Twitter.[86]

The Dow Jones Industrial Average closed at 19,827.25 on Trump's inauguration day. Since then, it has skyrocketed, setting hundreds of record highs and peaking at 26,616. Unfortunately for Eichenwald's kids, it looks like they'll be taking out student loans. Fortunately for Eichenwald's kids, $150,000 in debt for a useless "education" might just deter them from enrolling at an American university, in which case they will grow up to be significantly more intelligent than their father.

Eichenwald is more famous for his numerous controversial blunders than for his economic advice, thankfully. In April 2018, he got himself into trouble for lying about his affiliation with *Vanity Fair* and claiming that a teenaged survivor of the devastating Marjory Stoneman Douglas High School shooting, pro-Second Amendment activist Kyle Kashuv, was in "desperate need of psychiatric help or support." While making this claim via email, Eichenwald labeled himself as a contributing editor of *Vanity Fair*. But the magazine distanced itself from him, saying that he was no longer affiliated with *Vanity Fair*, and that he had not been affiliated with them for some time. Eichenwald claimed that he did not know that he had been let go from the magazine. Just a week prior, he had been forced to admit that he was also not a contributor at MSNBC, though his Twitter bio said otherwise.[87] The clown can't even figure out where he works. Why the hell would anyone trust him for any advice, financial or otherwise?

For some reason, Eichenwald is obsessed with making spurious claims about the mental health of those whom he views as political adversaries.

"I believe Trump was institutionalized in a mental hospital for a nervous breakdown in 1990, which is why he won't release medical records," he Tweeted in September 2016 while employed by *Newsweek*.[88] Eichenwald provided no evidence to support the claim, because there was none. He made it up. The Tweet was deleted shortly after it was posted. To Eichenwald's credit, *Newsweek* at least agreed that he was employed there during this controversy.

Most famously, Eichenwald was busted in March 2007 paying a source in exchange for a story.[89] The source and the subject of the story was a teenager named Justin Berry, who was exploited by adult men into running a child pornography site. The story ran in December 2015, and for it Eichenwald won the University of Oregon's Payne Award for Ethics in Journalism. Eichenwald accompanied the story with an essay published in *The New York Times* detailing how he came into contact with Berry, in which he described that he and the *Times* had personally helped Berry, who was suffering physically and emotionally from the trauma induced by his experiences, to get help from doctors. While Berry recovered, Eichenwald had helped him find an attorney to press charges against his abusers, and a friend of Eichenwald provided Berry with an apartment to stay in. During this series of events, Eichenwald convinced Berry to go public with the story, blurring ethical lines.

By January of the next year, the public was asking questions about Eichenwald's close personal relationship with Berry. When Berry took his abusers to court, filings showed that—unbeknownst to the *Times* and its readers—Eichenwald had paid Berry $2000 during their relationship, which is clearly unethical. Paying sources is frowned upon in the reporting business, for obvious reasons. Eichenwald's excuse for the payment was that he was acting as a private citizen, not a reporter, when he paid Berry. That is a lousy excuse considering that every reporter in existence is also a private citizen.

With such a history, would you be surprised that Eichenwald, a supposed "expert" in the field of political journalism, was wrong in his prediction that the stock market would crash under Trump?

There were plenty of other supposed "experts" in liberal media who were wrong about Trump's economy, too.

In an article titled "Economists: A Trump win would tank the markets,"[90] *Politico*'s chief economic correspondent Ben White predicted an economic doomsday in the event of a Trump election.

"Wall Street is set up for a major crash if Donald Trump shocks the world on Election Day and wins the White House,"

White's piece said. "New research out on Friday suggests that financial markets strongly prefer a Hillary Clinton presidency and could react with panicked selling should Trump defy the polls and deliver a shocking upset on Nov. 8."

The economists who conducted the study cited by White were Dartmouth College's Eric Zitzewitz and University of Michigan's Justin Wolfers. White noted that the research showed the stock market was worth 11 percent more under a Clinton presidency than a Trump presidency, which he described as "highly unusual" given that markets generally "prefer Republican policies on taxes, trade and regulations."

The Washington Post editorial board produced a steaming pile of manure on the potentials of a Trump economy, too, in a piece subtly titled "A President Trump could destroy the world economy."[91]

The piece began with a litany about the "global economy," and how, around the world, hundreds of millions of people in various countries like China, Indonesia, Egypt, India, and Brazil had seen economic prosperity since the end of the Cold War. *The Post* praised America's global trade policies for helping hundreds of millions of people worldwide achieve higher wages and move into the middle class, and insisted that the "United States needs to ensure that more of its own middle class shares in the benefits of globalization."

The paper then chastised Trump for calling for an end to the North American Free Trade Agreement (NAFTA) and threatening China with tariffs to bring back manufacturing jobs. *The Post*'s editorial board simply could not understand why Americans liked the idea of a leader who would focus on American prosperity instead of the prosperity of third world countries. While bragging about how well the middle class in Egypt was doing since the end of the Cold War, *The Post* totally forgot that wages for the American middle class had been largely stagnant since *before* the Cold War.[92]

Reading that article alone, you wouldn't guess that *The Post* was an American publication. Leave it to the doddering fools of *The Post's* editorial board, whose members live comfortably in their upscale urban palaces, to wonder why ordinary Americans might see value in a president who wanted them to be able to earn a modest living and provide for their families. Did they actually think the out-of-work machinist from Oklahoma gave a shit about the Indonesian economy? Had they considered that middle Americans whose jobs had been shipped overseas might want to get back to work? Of course not. Because they are completely out of touch with ordinary Americans. To *The Post's* editorial board, Oklahoma is just an annoying forty-five minutes of flight time between New York and Los Angeles.

More on such horrid economic reporting in a bit, but right around that time, the "experts" took a short break from being wrong about everything to watch in horror as Trump was elected as the forty-fifth President of the United States. Still, they were undeterred.

With the bevy of awful predictions before Trump's eventual victory, one might have reasonably expected the press to take a break from opinion-giving to get a clue before barfing up more nonsense. Unfortunately for all of us, that was not the case. On November 9, 2016, *The Washington Post* had the nerve to run an article titled "How Donald Trump Won: The Insiders Tell

Their Story." Those "insiders" must not have been available for comment at any time pre-election.

Since Trump's historic ascendance to the White House, the media has continued to make predictions, and they have continued to be wrong.

The New York Times' Paul Krugman, a supposed financial wiz, had some glum economic news for Americans in the wake of Trump's election.

"It really does now look like President Donald J. Trump, and markets are plunging," Krugman wrote in an article under the banner: "What Happened on Election Day,"[93] a series of articles about, well, what Paul Krugman thinks happened on Election Day. The specific article in which Krugman gave his dire warning was titled "The Economic Fallout."

"If the question is when markets will recover [from a Trump Presidency], a first-pass answer is never."

Never!

Through all of American history, markets have fallen and risen. But Krugman and the *Times* so despise Trump that they bet against the entirety of America's historical economic trends in an effort to smear him. The American economy survived the Great Depression of the 1930s, the financial collapse of 2008, and every peak and valley in between. But in Krugman's "expert" opinion, the American economy would not survive Trump.

Krugman offered no "second-pass answer"—no glimmer of hope that perhaps the economy would do poorly under Trump, but would eventually bounce back. That would be far too reasonable for a writer at the *Times*. The most charitable line of the entire piece was this: "Under any circumstances, putting an irresponsible, ignorant man who takes his advice from all the wrong people in charge of the nation with the world's most important economy would be very bad news."

What actually happened on election day turned out to be quite different from what Krugman, the "expert," told his readers happened on Election Day. The markets have chugged along just fine, what with the decreased taxes for businesses and ordinary Americans, massive cuts to costly and irritating federal government regulations, and hundreds of thousands of new jobs for those ordinary Americans to fill.

Filmmaker Michael Moore had some stock advice for ordinary Americans, too.

"I have no stocks. I advise people not to invest in the stock market, not now. Way too dangerous," he told *MarketWatch*.[94]

Krugman, Moore, and Eichenwald proved one thing for sure. It is advisable to accept investment tips and economic advice only from certified financial advisors. Liberal idiots with large Twitter followings are the last place to look for this type of advice.

As of September 2018, the American unemployment rate was 3.7 percent, its lowest since 1969, and annual pay for the average American worker had increased a solid 2.8 percent, according to the same *Washington Post* that swore up and down the Trump economy would be disastrous.[95] Unemployment was at 10 percent in 2009. *The Post* could not let Trump and the rest of America celebrate, though. They scolded him for sending a 6:06 a.m. Tweet breaking the good news to happily employed Americans who were just waking up to go to their new jobs, peevishly noting that he had broken a federal regulation dictating that "the president and members of the executive branch are not supposed to speak publicly about the jobs report until an hour after its 8:30 am release." Perhaps *The Post* has finally stumbled upon that impeachable offense they've been looking for after two years of spreading bogus lies about Russian "collusion."

Speaking of federal regulations, Trump slashed more than 34,000 of them between 2016 and 2017, many of which had killed jobs by hamstringing business owners and would-be entrepreneurs in red tape. In fact, small business owners spent an average of eighty hours and $83,000 per year complying with government mandates before Trump took office.[96] The regulations slash represents a savings of more than $1.3 billion to the federal government, or $15,000 in taxes per household.[97] Now if only he would do away with that one pesky regulation mandating he not discuss employment numbers before 9:30 a.m. on the day they're released, the *Washington Post* staff could rest easy.

When black unemployment fell to an all-time low of 5.9 percent in May 2018, most Americans celebrated. The writers at *Vox*, who are only arguably Americans, did not. They begrudgingly reported the news, but claimed there was a "catch."[98] The "catch" was that black unemployment was still higher than white unemployment, and as such, Trump is still a "racist." Just imagine the response had Obama presided over the lowest black unemployment rate in history. *Vox* would have crowned him king of America and ordained him as the second coming of Christ.

In July 2018, the Hispanic unemployment rate likewise hit an all-time low of 4.6 percent.[99] It's almost as though Trump's presidency has been positive for American minorities, whom those of us outside the race-baiting mainstream press usually just call "Americans."

How about those crash-and-burn economic predictions? The "experts" really nailed their thumbs to the wall on those.

In April 2017, shortly after Trump's inauguration, perpetually incorrect MSNBC contributor and *New York Magazine* columnist Josh Barro made a catalog of predictions about what Trump would *not* accomplish during his presidency, only to be proven wrong by December of the same year.[100] Among the agenda items that Barro claimed Trump would not touch were tax cuts, re-working the Affordable Care Act, and American trade policy. Shortly after Barro's publication, Trump enacted the largest tax cut in American history, eliminated the individual mandate that forced Americans to purchase healthcare from the government, and pulled out of the Trans-Pacific Partnership (TPP). In 2018, Trump further spited Barro by re-working the NAFTA.

Formerly relevant liberal commentator John Aravosis predicted a far more pessimistic outcome for the Trump presidency than a weakened economy.

"He'll be lucky if all we do is impeach him. I predict in 6 months Trump will be holed up in the Ecuadorian embassy," Aravosis said in a now-deleted Tweet, referencing WikiLeaks founder Julian Assange's current living situation.[101] Nearly two years later, Trump is resting comfortably in West Wing and Aravosis has egg on his face. In fact, Aravosis hasn't been heard from in a while. Maybe he's holed up somewhere with Bob Beckel. Or maybe with Assange as a new roommate.

Former *New York Times* columnist Tony Schwartz hedged his bets on Trump resigning by the end of 2017.

"I still believe (and pray) Trump will resign by year end to avoid worse humiliation - e.g. indictment by Mueller, or 25th amendment removal," he said on Twitter.[102]

In August 2017, Cenk Uygur of the inexplicably popular, Armenian genocide denying left-wing site *The Young Turks* assured the American public that Trump would be resigning in short order.

"He's done. You can write it down in stone. He will not finish his first term. There is no way in the world he finishes four years," Uygur said. "Now, as to how quickly that will happen—so that is a much harder guess. Like I said, definitely not the whole four years. It could be as quickly as a week, it could be as long as eighteen months."

Uygur eventually settled on a prediction of Trump's resignation "within six months" of August 2017. That mark has long since come to pass, and Trump is currently gearing up for his 2020 reelection bid.[103]

In May 2018, that pesky barrister Michael Avenatti, the object of the mainstream press's admiration, was making headlines again by claiming that Trump would resign before his first term was up.

"Ultimately, he is going to be forced to resign," Avenatti said. "I don't know how he will ultimately spin his departure, but I firmly believe there is going to be too much evidence of wrongdoing by him and those around him for him to be able to survive the balance of his term."[104]

There is always a chance that Trump could resign before January 2021, but at this point it looks like Avenatti's foray into politics will be far shorter than Trump's. The rumored 2020 Democratic candidate was later arrested for domestic violence, which does not poll especially well with decent people.[105] A week after that revelation, his client Stormy Daniels accused him of hiding the money that was raised for her through two GoFundMe campaigns after she levied a failed defamation lawsuit against President Trump. She also told the public that Avenatti filed the lawsuit without her consent in the first place, likely in an attempt to thrust himself into the national spotlight for political purposes.[106] After that debacle, he decided not to run for president in 2020 out of "respect for his family."[107] Avenatti's political career will likely begin and end with rumors that he was considering running for president.

The "experts" in the mainstream media are generally wrong about everything. If they were wrong about a few small, unimportant things from time to time, the American public might be capable of giving them some leeway. Unfortunately, the press makes wildly far-fetched predictions about near-impossible events like Trump's resignation, or stock market collapses, making it impossible to take them seriously.

But they proceed this way because the tiny percentage of leftist radicals to whom they are trying to appeal want to hear it. That way, the radical leftist crowd can log onto their little echo chambers on social media or Reddit and pretend to be insiders with foreknowledge of what is to come. Monumental predictions made by D.C. "insiders," the least trustworthy people on earth, sell advertisements. As long as there is a demand from that tiny portion of radicals, the grave and awful predictions will keep coming. Regardless of how many times the "experts" are proven wrong, page views and viewership will always come first. Plausibility, rationality, and common-sense matter not to the corporate press. Cash is king. The only thing that matters is profit.

CHAPTER 5

SEX CRAZED

If you hadn't noticed, much of the mainstream press has been reduced to single, mid-thirties, urban socialites bitching about the repercussions of their own sexual promiscuity, or more specifically their sex lives, sexual preferences, sexual identities, sexual organs, sexual positions, and anything else sex-related that once-serious news outlets have lowered their standards to publish.

In September 2018, *The New York Times*, formerly the "paper of record," printed an op-ed by a woman named Courtney Sender. It was titled "He Asked Permission to Touch, but Not to Ghost."[108]

Sparing the cringeworthy details, the gist of the piece was that Sender invited a Tinder match to her apartment for a "first date," and he asked her about a hundred times for consent before, during, and after their sexual encounter. He asked "Is this okay?" before taking off every article of clothing and before every sexual act. Sender was confused by the encounter.

"It seemed legalistic and self-protective, imported more from the courtroom than from a true sense of caretaking," she wrote. "And each time he asked, it was as if he assumed I lacked the agency to say no on my own—as if he expected me to say no, not believing that a woman would have the desire to keep saying yes."

She sought to understand the man's behavior by inviting him over for another "date." They had sex a second a time, and then he never called her again.

For the rest of the piece, she groused about her personal loneliness, and how America's culture of consent is "too narrow." Consent, Sender argued, should extend to actually caring about the person with whom one is intimate.

The culture for which Sender longs does exist. Some people do not invite "first dates" to their homes for inevitable hookups. Ordinary people might argue that not sleeping with someone on a "first date" is an easy way to avoid such dissatisfying experiences. Some people actually take time to build trusting relationships before sexual intimacy, ensuring that their partner does not simply walk out, never to be seen again. These people are generally conservatives and Christians. And the "progressive" media calls these people regressive prudes. Stories about respectful relationships aren't sexy enough to make into the pages of the *Times*. Because sex sells, American media has made young people sex-crazed, and consequently Sender is on the short lists for future cat ladies and *New York Times* columnists, respectively. The state of our media has been so far degraded that rants about awkward sexual encounters now fill its pages. It's pathetic.

Nearly everything in the mainstream press is centered around sex. The *New York Times* opinion page has become barely distinguishable from *Cosmopolitan* magazine. Be on the lookout for "Twenty-One Sex Tips to Drive Your Man Wild" by Paul Krugman in this week's *Times* Sunday editorials.

Case in point, recently *Cosmopolitan* actually wrote a response critiquing a *New York Times* opinion piece called "The Redistribution of Sex," wherein former conservative turned Trump hater Ross Douthat argued that postmodern culture has seen the most sex bestowed upon the wealthy and good-looking, thus resulting in a culture of "incel" or involuntarily celibate men who need other outlets for procuring sexual activity.[109] Douthat's argument was not novel, inasmuch as this has been the arrangement between men and women for the entire history of mankind. (Bear in mind that Douthat is one of the more impressive columnists over at the *Times*.) Further, he argued that there is a void in the marketplace for sex which will be filled by legalized prostitution, sex robots, and pornography. Perhaps the *Times* should have categorized this piece in the "economics" section, as Douthat seems to have a better grasp on supply and demand than most of the paper's economic "experts."

"Whether sex workers and sex robots can actually deliver real fulfillment is another matter. But that they will eventually be asked to do it, in service to a redistributive goal that for now still seems creepy or misogynist or radical, feels pretty much inevitable," Douthat wrote.

The man-hating third-wave feminists at *Cosmopolitan* took offense to Douthat's column, likely because he was treading on their territory by writing a raunchy, morally degenerate article, and a turf war ensued.

ENEMIES

Moira Donegan fired back at the *Times* with an article of her own, titled "Actually, We Don't Owe You Sex And We Never Will."[110] She argued that Douthat is an incel, sex is not a commodity to be traded for, and that incels are simply looking for an excuse to "rape on demand." Douthat may well be an incel, but it seems that Donegan has forgotten that prostitution is one of the oldest trades in history. As for the "rape on demand" claim, third-wave feminists have a tenuous relationship with the reality of men, at best, wherein they believe that every man is born a rapist. The vast majority of us, of course, make it through life managing never to rape. Some of us even have standards. For example, I would never sleep with a *Cosmopolitan* columnist for fear of sexually transmitted dull-wittedness.

Cosmopolitan's pissing contest with the once-revered *New York Times* over sexual behavior of lonely men is a perfect barometer for the American press's historic fall from grace. The ordinary American who barely has time to catch the evening news is not reading that crap. Donegan and Douthat might as well be talking to themselves. But sex still sells among the cosmopolitan elite who have time on their hands and want all the gushy details, and thus the stories keep coming.

In November 2018, the *Times* ran another incredible piece by transgender woman Andrea Long Chu called "My New Vagina Won't Make Me Happy."[111]

"Next Thursday, I will get a vagina," she said. "The procedure will last around six hours, and I will be in recovery for at least three months. Until the day I die, my body will regard the vagina as a wound; as a result, it will require regular, painful attention to maintain. This is what I want, but there is no guarantee it will make me happier. In fact, I don't expect it to. That shouldn't disqualify me from getting it."

This fascinating content, by the way, is unlimited with the *Times'* one dollar/week subscription deal, which always seems to be ending soon, but has never actually ended.

HuffPost loves to write about sex, too. It actually began as an online tabloid before attempting to pivot into serious journalism. Whether that pivot was successful is up for debate. Still, any sex stories it can find, it will publish. Like a recent piece called "What It's Like to Date When You're Asexual."[112] Asexual people, called "aces," apparently do not feel sexually attracted to anyone.

Kim, a twenty-four-year-old manager at the Astraea Lesbian Foundation for Justice in New York City, was profiled for the piece.

"I'm non-binary and I consider myself asexual and demi-panromantic (though for me, I'm also fine with other non-monosexual/romantic labels like 'bi' and 'queer'). I use "asexual" as a label because I don't really experience sexual attraction," she said.

I don't know what that sentence means, and I suspect most of you don't either. Apparently, Kim's love life is complicated.

She describes in the piece how utterly annoying it is to explain to simpletons like you and I why she wants to date even though she does not feel sexually attracted to people. Then she seamlessly transitions into explaining that sometimes she does have sex and sometimes she does feel sexually attracted to people. Maybe I'm not enlightened enough to be the subject of a *HuffPost* piece on sex, but it seems to me that Kim could just be described as "choosy."

You might be under the impression that the press only publishes stories of gripping sexual encounters exclusively between human beings. Think again. A 2014 *New York Magazine* headline proves that if this was your sincerely held belief, you were sadly, painfully mistaken.

A piece titled "What It's Like to Date a Horse," written by Alexa Tsoulis-Reay, intimately described the sex life of a forty-two-year-old Canadian man who refers to himself as a "zoophile."[113]

"I started to notice horses in 'that' way when I was about 11 or 12," the man said. "Everybody else was stealing their dads' *Playboy* magazines, but I had a book called *The Big Book of the Horse*."

The article is an absolute goldmine of depravity wherein the man describes his awkward adolescence, taking a female (human) to the prom, and subsequently losing his virginity to a horse at age twenty-two. Asked how he found his first partner, he divulged the following:

"One of my friends had access to a nice female pony, and he let me have sex with her. She was a Shetland-cross, and she had dorsal stripes—the black line across the spine—and that's something that's turned me on ever since."

I'll spare any further details about this particular gentleman's sex life in case you have a weak stomach. For inquiring minds, though, "zoophiles" are generally monogamous. They choose a steady partner and cohabitate with it like you would with your human partner.

Of all of the words in the history of the English language that have been, and can be, strung together to convey beautiful thoughts, colorful imagery, and deeply philosophical beliefs, the 21st century American press manages to consistently assemble words in such a manner that puts its readers in danger of hurling up their lunch. It is truly a talent.

When the media is not busy indulging us in the detailed sex life of every interested participant, their latest focus has been President Trump's sex life.

The Stormy Daniels story dominates the news cycle when more important stories like made-up Russian "collusion" or calls for Trump's impeachment over his love of Diet Coke[114] are not timely.

A brief refresher for my readers who do not own televisions, have access to the internet, or were fortunate enough to enter a vegetative state prior to this ordeal: Daniels, a pornographic film actress known for her roles in such cinematic masterpieces as "Love Potion 69," "Porking With Pride 2," and "Trailer Trash Nurses 6,"[115] whose real name is Stephanie Clifford, claims that she had sex with Trump in an extramarital affair in 2006. She also claims that she was paid $130,000 to keep quiet about the affair and that the payment was made by Michael Cohen, Trump's former personal attorney. She sued the president to be relieved of her obligations under an apparent non-disclosure agreement, and had a defamation suit against the president tossed by a judge.[116]

The press has been known to drag her out of whatever filthy strip club she is performing in, slap a pantsuit on her, and roll her out in front of a national audience. Daniels appeared on the once-revered news program "60 Minutes," which landed the first interview with her after the affair allegations went public. She has also been booked on "The View" and "Jimmy Kimmel Live."

Daniels even penned a book about her sexcapades with Trump (good work if you can get it) called "Full Disclosure," and the press had a feeding frenzy when *The Guardian* obtained an advanced copy before it was released. The press went straight for the kill. Every article featured the climax of Daniels' salacious literary work: her description of Trump's genitalia.

"She describes Trump's penis as 'smaller than average' but 'not freakishly small,'" the *Guardian* piece said. "'He knows he has an unusual penis.... It has a huge mushroom head. Like a toadstool...I lay there, annoyed that I was getting fucked by a guy with Yeti pubes and a dick like the mushroom character in Mario Kart.... It may have been the least impressive sex I'd ever had, but clearly, he didn't share that opinion.'"[117]

Playboy has never featured such a vulgar article. But the mainstream press? They reported on the shape and size of Trump's member with glee. One can only imagine middle-aged know-nothing reporters giggling over it in their editorial meetings.

The only person the press loves more than Stormy herself is her attorney, Michael Avenatti. He is a world-class huckster, and as such attracts a fantastic amount of media. He even earned himself the nickname "Creepy Porn Lawyer" in certain circles.

During a sixty-four-day period from March 7 to May 10, Avenatti appeared on CNN at least sixty-five times and MSNBC forty-three times. Avenatti had certain go-to programs where he was booked over and over again. Every leftist news network in America wanted a piece of the Avenatti action. He was interviewed twenty times on Anderson Cooper's "AC 360," eight times on CNN's "Tonight with Don Lemon," twenty times on CNN's "New Day," fourteen times on MSNBC's "The Last Word with Lawrence O'Donnell," and seven times on MSNBC's "Deadline: White House."[118] He averaged more than one segment per day on CNN during that time period.

Avenatti made it a point to avoid any media outlets that are politically right of Stalin, but after months of invitations, he finally agreed to appear live in Fox's "Tucker Carlson Tonight."

While Carlson drilled down into Avenatti's potential 2020 run for president, his millions of dollars in free press coverage, and asked if Avenatti felt that he was exploiting his client, Daniels, by using the press to make himself a national figure while she continued to work a pole in strip clubs, Avenatti quickly turned the interview into a hypersexualized circus, making it a referendum on watching pornography. But Avenatti's line of questioning is exactly what leftist news outlets, which are barely one step above Kardashian-esque reality television, love to discuss. Ordinary Americans watching Fox were disgusted. For Avenatti, it was just another day at the office. Here is an excerpt from the transcript of the interview:[119]

> *Avenatti: Do you have that big a problem with porn? When's the last time you've saw porn?*
>
> *Carlson: Oh, you busted me. Actually, I'm into humiliation porn, that's why I watch you on CNN.*
>
> *Avenatti: But when's the last time you've viewed porn?*

Carlson: You're a little creepier even than I realized.... You're dodging the question that I have asked you repeatedly.

Avenatti: Do you have a problem with porn? What's the problem with porn? Let me ask you a question: Do you believe that people who view porn should watch your show?

It was baffling.

By the end of May, Avenatti had done 164 total cable news appearances and received $175 million worth of free press[120]— all to discuss the sex life of his porn star client. None of this benefitted his client, but night after night, Avenatti was piped into America's collective living room. Willing dupes who still watch cable news were mainlining sleaziness courtesy of the cable news. It was segment after segment of smear after smear against Trump for his alleged past sexual encounters. The press and their dwindling audience ate it up, while no one else gave a hoot.

CNN and their counterparts are out of touch with ordinary Americans, and as such seem to have missed the fact that nobody elected Trump to be their moral or spiritual guide. For that, conservatives go to church, rather than looking to government, shady attorneys, or primetime news anchors.

While cable news continues to delude itself, thinking that it is one Trump sex scandal away from its ultimate goal of helping the Democrat party impeach him, Trump voters and conservatives at large simply do not care. After all, this is a billionaire real estate mogul that we're talking about. Voters, including the coveted evangelical Christian demographic, knew that when they went to the polls in 2016, and they elected him anyway. Nobody expects Trump to be chaste, except the morons in the mainstream press who feign outrage over everything, especially Trump's sexual promiscuity. The same people who fill their pages and make the big bucks pushing "sex positivity" and encouraging young people to hump anything that walks want to lecture us about Trump's morality? Nobody is buying it.

If anything, the "Trump banged a porn star" narrative only impressed his base. It may have briefly shocked suburban mothers and the #resist crowd (not that they are in a position to lecture anyone on morality, either), but after years of boring, weak-kneed establishment Republicans dominating the GOP—impotent Bushes, wimps like Ohio Governor John Kasich, and five-foot-nothing virgins like Sen. Marco Rubio (R-FL)—Trump's base likely reveled in his alleged sexual conquest with an adult film actress. "Finally, someone who can get laid!" they likely thought.

It certainly did not hurt his poll numbers. His weekly average approval rating was actually higher in 2018 than it was in 2017 before the Daniels allegations and hours of wall-to-wall press coverage.[121]

When the Avenatti coverage died down a bit, America soon became gripped by the most polarizing Supreme Court nomination in modern history. Justice Brett Kavanaugh, formerly of the United States Court of Appeals for the District of Columbia—known as the second most important court in America after the Supreme Court itself—was under intense scrutiny for patently unprovable allegations of sexual misconduct made by a high school acquaintance of his, stemming from an alleged incident that took place in the early 1980s while the pair was in high school. Actually, that was about the extent of the details of the allegation. But the press ran with it, making a mockery out of journalistic integrity in the process.

Kavanaugh's accuser, Christine Blasey Ford, is a leftist professor from Palo Alto, California, who did not remember when the alleged incident occurred, where it occurred, how she got to or from wherever it occurred, most of the people who were present at the gathering where it allegedly occurred, and had zero corroborating witnesses. In fact, her best friend, who was supposedly at the gathering, had no recollection of it whatsoever.

The story would be altogether unremarkable if the subject had not been Justice Kavanaugh. A prominent sex crimes prosecutor even said that she would have no basis to obtain as much as a search warrant based on Ford's recollection of events, or lack thereof.[122]

Unfortunately for Kavanaugh, who boasts an impeccable record of exemplary conduct during his thirty years of public service, the story combined the media's two favorite things: Sex and destroying Republicans. It resulted in an absolute media feeding frenzy while the Republican-controlled Senate balked, calling for an FBI investigation into the matter after Kavanaugh had passed through six previous FBI background checks with flying colors.

On September 14, after the judge had sailed through his confirmation hearing and just before he was scheduled to be confirmed, *The New Yorker* published a bare bones account of the alleged sexual misconduct without naming Ford, who had requested anonymity. This piqued the media's curiosity, and like a pack of hungry wild dogs, they chased down the source of the story. Two days later, Ford went public with her allegations in an interview with *The Washington Post*. Ford recounted in Senate testimony that the press had staked out her home, knocking on her doors and windows and even harassing her dog before she finally gave into their pressure and accepted a public interview. Anything for a juicy sex story!

With Kavanaugh's confirmation delayed, the media went into seek-and-destroy mode. CNN producer Scott Bronstein was even caught on audiotape cold-calling Kavanaugh's Yale classmates in an attempt to dig up dirt against Kavanaugh.[123]

When a second accuser, Deborah Ramirez, contacted *The New Yorker*, she originally declined to provide details about her allegations because her memory "contained gaps." But after six days of huddling with her attorney, she reached back out to *The New Yorker* who ran with a piece claiming that Kavanaugh had "thrust his penis into her face, and caused her to touch it without consent."[124] The story was so salacious and unverifiable (Ramirez also provided no corroborating witnesses) that even *The New York Times*, who weeks earlier had run an anonymous opinion piece written by a high-level government employee who claimed that many people in the Trump administration were working against him,[125] refused to run the story. Anonymous opinion pieces are unheard of. In fact, I could not find a single other instance of a news outlet publishing an anonymous opinion piece. Even with that considered, the Ramirez story was too rich for the *Times'* blood.

Finally, a third accuser came forward against Kavanaugh. Re-enter the creepy porn lawyer, Avenatti. Through the unsavory barrister, a woman named Julie Swetnick released a statement claiming that she had witnessed multiple efforts on behalf of Kavanaugh and his friends to get teenage girls "inebriated and disoriented so they could then be 'gang raped' in a side room or bedroom by a 'train' of numerous boys."[126] The allegation fell flat on its face when Swetnick claimed that she had attended upwards of ten of these so-called "gang rape" parties. Hundreds of conservative pundits asked a simple question that blew the lid off the narrative: why would Swetnick attend *multiple* parties where she knew drugging and abusive gang rapes would occur? The story might have been believable had she claimed that she attended one such party and was too afraid to ever return. But the story was made up, and small details like these fall through the cracks when scumbag lawyers team up with unseemly women to assail the character of a political figure in a last-ditch effort to keep power. Swetnick also provided no corroborating witnesses, like the other accusers.

As expected, the mainstream press completely ignored the nuance, and instead invited their favorite guest back on air to discuss the allegations. In an interview with Avenatti the day after Kavanaugh was bullied into admitting that he was a virgin throughout high school and "for many years after," CNN's Chris Cuomo and Avenatti speculated in primetime about what exactly Kavanaugh meant:[127]

Cuomo: "Kavanaugh says, 'I never had sex in high school. Never had sex afterwards.'"[128]

Avenatti: "What exactly is he saying? Is he saying that he did not have sexual intercourse? Are we going to get into a definition of sexual intercourse? Does that mean that he performed oral sex or had oral sex performed on him? Does that mean any host of any other sexual activities occurred? Or does he want America to believe that the only thing that he did until well into his college years was effectively kissed or French kissed a woman?"

What else could Kavanaugh have possibly meant? Kavanaugh saying "I never had sex in high school" left very little room for interpretation. No one else had questions about that statement except for hard-hitting reporters at CNN. Unsatisfied, Cuomo just had to invite Avenatti onto his program to flesh it out further. And flesh it out they did, to the disgust of ordinary people everywhere.

After Ford testified in front of the Senate Judiciary Committee, the media gave her "credibility" ringing endorsements. Despite the complete lack of evidence, she *sounded* sincere, they said. Kavanaugh, too, had the opportunity to testify in an effort to clear his name. He was visibly upset, and defiantly answered petty questions from U.S. Senators about inside jokes written in his high school yearbook at age sixteen. After his hearing, the press ran hundreds of articles saying that Kavanaugh's testimony proved that he lacked the temperament to sit on the bench of the Supreme Court. The man had just been falsely accused of gang rape! He had been forced to discuss the most intimate details of life on national television! Of course he was angry! The press acted like the grade-school bully who would throw a dodgeball at your face, beat you up, stuff you in a locker, and then ask "Oh, are you mad? What are you so mad about?"

Leftist mainstream press outlets have made millions of dollars in advertising revenue by cranking out segments and think-pieces about the sex lives of ordinary Americans and political high-brows alike. The entire media apparatus has whored itself out to advertisers with the promise of turning their "news" shows into evening versions of the *Jerry Springer Show*. In fact, in the current climate, Springer could probably land himself a cable news show in primetime. Who would notice the difference between the content from back in the heyday of his show and what passes for "news" in 2019?

It is the oldest adage in media: sex sells. The mainstream press would rather contribute to the degeneration of our society than actually inform anyone about anything. It is one of the many reasons they should be considered an enemy of the people.

CHAPTER 6

THEY FELL FOR IT

Every year in America, there are hundreds of hate crimes reported by the mainstream press. Whenever a hate crime occurs, the press plays the role of America's moral conscience, often delivering somber lectures about how hurtful such actions are. They do so while hiding a smirk. You see, the press loves hate crimes—particularly hate crimes where Democrats get to play the victim. This allows them to further promulgate their narrative about "right wing extremism," and one good hate crime story foments enough anger among their leftist audiences to sell plenty of advertisements. Unlike regular, more boring crimes, hate crimes are usually inherently political. So, Democrats borrow a page out of the book of the mayor of Chicago, Rahm Emanuel, who once said to "never let a good crisis go to waste."[129] They hype these crimes up, inevitably associating them with the Republican Party, or President Trump, or both.

The problem, though, is that oftentimes hate crimes are faked for political gain, particularly by leftists who lack a moral compass. Orchestrating fake hate crimes and letting the press run wild is a tried and true tactic of the political left. By the time the perpetrator of the crime is found to have made it up, the public at large has focused its attention on something else, and the press has already received the viewership and page views that pay their salaries. Rarely does the leftist media give an update to tell their viewership that they were mistaken. Why bother with that when the checks are already cashed? As an added benefit, they give a little boost to their friends in the Democratic Party. Hate crime hoaxes occur so frequently that there is an entire website dedicated to documenting them.[130]

The hate crime hoax that provoked the most hideous and irresponsible media attacks against President Trump and the political right was the series of Jewish community center bomb threat hoaxes in early 2017. Thousands of bomb threats were called into Jewish community centers across the United States, as well as airports, schools, and political offices. Immediately the press jumped at the opportunity to blame Trump.

The hoaxes were recklessly ascribed to the "alt-right," a term that used be synonymous with neo-Nazis, but has since become synonymous with all Trump supporters thanks to mainstream press slander. *Slate* writer Elissa Strauss said in the left-wing rag:

> *For many on the alt-right, the taunts and threats they issue—possibly including the ones aimed at the JCCs— are an elaborate practical joke. But, as the* New Yorker's *Emily Nussbaum points out in her analysis of the rise of Trump and his fellow reactionaries through the lens of*

comedy, these jokes aren't benign. Taunting, as bullies have long known, makes a wily tool of oppression. Should the object of the joke protest the humor, they are written off as uptight and the bully is emboldened. Ignore it and, yep, the bully is still emboldened.[131]

Trump was also targeted by the press for what it viewed as a tepid response to the situation.

"The White House in particular had been a target of criticism for its response -- or the lack of one. The President did mention the threats in his speech Tuesday evening, but did not outline a plan to stop them," CNN said.[132]

The perpetrator turned out to be a dual Israeli-American citizen and teenager who made the threats from his home in a small town in Israel. When he was captured with the help of the FBI, nobody in the mainstream press bothered to apologize to Trump or his supporters after blaming them for terrorism. Eventually, the teen was sentenced to ten years in prison for the threats, which had nothing to do with anti-Semitism, and everything to do with the perpetrator being mentally ill.[133]

Four days before the midterm elections in 2018, a synagogue in Brooklyn was vandalized with anti-Semitic graffiti. Messages, including "Kill all Jews" were found scrawled on the walls of the synagogue in permanent marker just before the venue was set to host a Democrat rally, headlined by "Broad City" star Ilana Glazer. Glazer was set to interview State Senate candidates Andrew Gounardes of South Brooklyn and Jim Gaughran of Long Island, both Democrats.

"Tonight's attack, right here in a temple in Brooklyn – is a painful reminder that anti-Semitism and prejudice are alive and well in our own community," Gounardes wrote in a statement, as reported by CBS.[134]

Predictably, left wingers in the press immediately blamed Trump, and those who did not specifically mention Trump by name likened "white supremacy" with the Republican Party, as is commonplace in media.

"This happened last night in NYC - this is TRUMP'S AMERICA," *Daily Beast* columnist Dean Obeidallah Tweeted to his 81,000 followers, attaching a link to one of the hundreds of articles written about the event.[135]

Miami Herald columnist Lesley Abravanel Tweeted a list of anti-Semitic events at Trump, including the synagogue vandalism, shortly after the event, as if to lay the blame at his feet.[136]

A day later, police arrested a suspect in the hate crime. His name was James Polite, a self-described "queer" African-American male, and adoptee of two Jewish parents. He was also a Democrat who worked for Barack Obama's 2008 campaign.[137]

Those mainstream press outlets that bothered to update their original stories to reflect Polite's arrest made no connection between him and the Obama campaign or the Democratic Party. That does not fit the preferred narrative. So, their audiences carried on in ignorance, and their anger for the political right festered. Twitter was still abuzz with talks of "right-wing anti-Semitism" stemming from the incident through Tuesday, November 6—midterm election day in 2018. Mission accomplished for the propaganda arm of the DNC.

Hate crime hoaxes come in many shapes and sizes. For example, a teenaged Texas waiter duped the dimwitted press with ease, likely not expecting anyone—never mind damn near the entire American media apparatus—what with their fancy journalism degrees, nose for the truth, and steadfast commitment to publishing only provable facts, to pick up on his little stunt. But his little stunt, as it turned out, was right up their alley.

"'We Don't Tip Terrorist': Customer Banned from Texas Restaurant after Leaving Server Racist Note," read a headline from *The Root* in June 2018.[138]

The Root, a far-from-fringe black supremacist website, filed the story under a category called "Trump's America." Several other mainstream press sites, including *USA Today* and the *New York Post*, reported on the event.

"At the moment I didn't know what to think nor what to say, I was sick to my stomach. I share this because I want people to understand that this racism, and this hatred still exists," the alleged victim, Khalil Cavil, wrote on his Facebook page, where he attached a photo of the note. "Although, this is nothing new, it is still something that will test your faith. All day I've had to remind myself that Jesus died for these people too."

The chief operating officer of Saltgrass Steakhouse, where Cavil was employed, immediately banned the customer from the restaurant for life.

KMID, the local ABC news affiliate in the Texas basin, platformed Cavil immediately, interviewing him and helping to promote his sob story. The story made great television, after all. How could anyone look at the clean-cut, innocent looking kid and not feel badly for him? ABC could hear the cash register ca-chinging from the ads it would sell after running with the story.

"My heart just dropped, I didn't know what to say or what to think in the moment but there's hurt there," Khalil told the station in an interview. "My dad was in the military and a buddy that he was very close to, served with him...Khalil was killed in an accident and so my dad just named me after him, one of his best friends."[139]

Alas, there was one minor problem. Three days later, Cavil admitted to fabricating the whole story. He wrote the racist note on the bill himself. After news broke that he fabricated the entire incident, the story was buried by mainstream press. No one bothered to interview Cavil to ask him why he would stir up racial divisiveness. *The Washington Post* wrote a softball follow-up, in which it begrudgingly printed the following:

"The incident came amid increased attention given to incidents of racist behavior in the public sphere, particularly as they are shared in social media posts that generate thousands of views and strong emotions. But the ease with which fake information can spread on the Internet before it is ever verified remains a persistent concern."[140]

Notice they shifted the blame from themselves and the rest of the mainstream press, all of whom ran with the story without verifying that the racist note was real, to "social media posts that generate thousands of views." You know what else generates thousands of views? Mainstream press reporting—even when they shirk their responsibility to check the facts. They fell for it.

A hotbed for hoaxed hate crimes in America is the university campus. No longer open forums for the free exchange of ideas or institutions of higher education, university campuses have become radical leftist indoctrination camps and daycare centers for overgrown children. As such, they are breeding grounds for just the type of environment where hate crime hoaxes flourish.

American universities are unique in that victimhood status equates to a certain social clout. Victimhood groups, in descending order of importance, are as follows: Blacks, Latinos, all other minorities, religious minorities, transgender people, gays and lesbians, disabled people, and females. Of course, it is possible to be a member of more than one of these victimhood groups. In such situations, one's social clout increases exponentially, sort of like the double letter score in a game of Scrabble. For example, a black lesbian female holds more social clout on an American college campus than a white lesbian female, and so forth. The more social clout one owns, the more one's opinion matters in public discourse. Way down at the bottom of the social clout list is the straight, white, Christian male. And God forbid he's a Republican.

So, when a member of a victimhood group with enormous social clout claims to have been a victim of a hate crime, universities stop the presses. Actually, they start the presses. Blame the straight, white, Christian males and Republicans first, ask questions later. Allow me to illustrate with a few documented cases:

A Bowling Green State University student falsely identified a piece of lab equipment covered by a white sheet that she saw through a window as a member of the Ku Klux Klan.

"There's been an active KKK group in Bowling Green, OH since 1922," the student Tweeted at the university and its president, causing a social media firestorm. "soo, how does this promote diversity &a [sic] inclusion?"[141]

She attached a photo of the "KKK member."

Rather embarrassingly for the student, the university's president tweeted back at her, informing her of her mistake, and assuring her that the Klan wouldn't be burning any crosses at BGSU.

A few days after Trump's election to the presidency, a Muslim female at San Diego State University claimed that she was beaten, her hijab ripped off, and her car stolen by a group of white males who allegedly told her, "Now that Trump is president get ready to start fleeing." Those with a semblance of common sense might question such a far-fetched story, given its timing and the oddly direct messaging of the alleged perpetrators. But common sense is not a prerequisite to attend or lecture at an American university. Not to mention, questioning such a story from someone with such a high level of social clout would not be politically correct. Questioning someone's victimhood status is a certain way to get blackballed from higher education.

San Diego's trusty newspaper, the *Union-Tribune*, reported on the tragic hate crime,[142] as did San Diego's NBC affiliate.[143]

A Muslim student at San Diego State University was robbed Wednesday by two men who made comments "about President-elect Trump and the Muslim community," according to a police statement. Her car also was stolen following the incident. The woman was wearing traditional Muslim clothing, including a hijab, when she was robbed about 2:30 p.m. in a parking structure at the Campanile Drive campus. According to campus police, the woman was confronted in the [sic] a stairwell where the men grabbed her purse and backpack, took her keys and fled.

In reality, the student had forgotten where she parked her car. She made up the entire story to avoid copping to her own stupidity. Only eight months later did she admit to the fabrication, and she was never punished. Neither the *Union-Tribune* nor NBC bothered to update their stories. There must have been too many other hate crime hoaxes to report.

In March 2017, a progressive group called the "Diversity Leadership Council," at Gustavus Adolphus College in Minnesota, hung posters all over campus with messages encouraging white students to report minorities to U.S. Customs and Immigration Enforcement (ICE).[144]

"A notice to all white Americans. It is your civil duty to report any and all illegal aliens to U.S. Customs and Immigration Enforcement. They are criminals. America is a white nation," the posters read.

The group weaseled its way out of the hate crime hoax by claiming that the posters were simply "meant to start a dialogue on discrimination, hate and bias." CBS Minnesota ate that story up, calling it a "social justice experiment."[145]

The Washington Post had a field day with a fake hate crime hoax at St. Olaf College in Minnesota in May 2017. A black student claimed to have received a menacing, racially charged note from an alleged "white supremacist." The note in question said, "I am so glad you are leaving soon. One less n***** this school has to deal with. You have spoken up too much. You will change nothing. Shut up or I will shut you up."[146]

The note sparked such intense backlash that the entire school shut down for a day. Students walked out of class, gathered in protest, and denounced the university as a whole. In order to get them back to class, the administration was embarrassingly forced to negotiate with, and eventually give in to the demands of the school's social justice club. *The Post* cheered them on, documenting the event in great detail.[147]

> *Following days of demonstrations against hate speech at a liberal arts college in Minnesota, the school has reached an agreement with student protesters. St. Olaf College President David Anderson sent an email to students late Monday stating that the administration had agreed with the student-led group "Collective For Change on The Hill," which interrupted a college forum earlier in the day to present administrators with their demands.*
>
> *"This is the first step in a process towards a long-term solution, and all of us on campus are committed to moving forward in a spirit of collaboration to address these important issues."*

Shortly thereafter, it was determined that the note was written by the alleged victim, who confessed to the scam. The school's president then informed the student body that the threat was not "genuine."

Ten days later, *The Washington Post* quietly updated their original story with a link to a newer, shorter story, reluctantly reporting that the whole thing was a hoax. Still, if you Google search the incident, the original *Post* story is at the top of the results list.

At Kansas State University, a black student was not charged for filing a false report after it turned out that he graffitied his own car with racist language. The man spray-painted messages like "Go Home N***** Boy," "Date Your Own Kind," and "Die." The Associated Press wrote a tearful story about the "victim" before his charade was unmasked.[148]

> *A black student whose car was scrawled with racist graffiti says he has withdrawn from Kansas State University as a result of the incident. The student who owns the car told the Kansas City Star in an interview that the vandalism and resulting social media attention has made it impossible for him to go anywhere in Manhattan, the home of the university. He said that he does not want the attention, has withdrawn from the university and will return to his home in California.*
>
> *"I was not raised to discriminate," he said. He called the vandalism "sad, hurtful and disappointing."*

AP described the "racist graffiti" as "the latest in a string of such incidents at the school," citing a previous incident during which students found a noose hanging from a tree on campus. That turned out to be a hoax, too.[149] AP, the world's foremost wire news service, never updated its story to reflect the fact that the event was staged.

Students are not the only ones on college campuses making up fake hate crimes. The esteemed brain trust of academics who are responsible for the education of our youth are also looking to get a piece of that sweet victimhood action. After all, every professor wants to be the "cool" professor.

In March 2017, fifty-two-year-old Azhar Hussain, an assistant professor of aviation technology at Indiana State University, filed a report with police after allegedly receiving emails that were both personally threatening and threatening to the Muslim community at large at ISU. Later in the same month, Hussain reported that he was physically attacked while entering his office and thrown to the floor. He said that he was attacked from behind, and that he could not see his alleged attackers. In fact, nobody was able to identify the culprits, and potential corroborating witnesses reported seeing nothing out of the ordinary.[150]

After a lengthy police investigation, it was determined that Hussain conjured up the entire narrative. He was arrested and booked on a felony charge of obstruction of justice, a misdemeanor charge of harassment and charges of making false reports. He was also blasted by ISU's chief of police, who was rightfully less than diplomatic in delivering the news of Hussain's arrest.

"Based upon the investigation, it is our belief that Hussain was trying to gain sympathy by becoming a victim of anti-Muslim threats which he had created himself," Chief Joseph Newport said. "It is extremely unfortunate that this situation caused undue concern on other members of the ISU community," he continued, annoyedly adding that the ISU police had wasted a great deal of resources sending out campus crime alerts after Hussain's falsified attacks.

If, at this point, you're coming to the conclusion that college campuses may not be the intellectual gathering places of old, you are correct.

But hate crime hoaxes happen elsewhere, too.

In June 2017, a Muslim woman from Des Moines, Iowa set fire to her own mosque, which sparked nationwide outrage. Police confirmed only days later that the incident was not a hate crime after they caught twenty-two-year-old Aisha Ismail on surveillance video sprinkling lighter fluid on the floor of the mosque and setting it alight.[151] But the most detestable element to that hate crime hoax would not occur until August, nearly two months later.

CNN ran the headline "On average, 9 mosques have been targeted every month this year."[152]

"We mapped 63 publicly reported incidents from January to July 2017, where mosques were targets of threats, vandalism or arson. On average, that comes down to nine every month and at least two a week," the news network proudly declared.

Conveniently, CNN decided to list mosque threats and attacks beginning in the same month that Trump was inaugurated. They weren't even attempting to be subtle in their scare mongering. The insinuation was obvious. CNN was telling its readers that America had become a more hateful country under Republican leadership, particularly Trump's leadership. And, wouldn't you know, they included the mosque arson in Des Moines on their list, knowing certainly that the arson that took place there was a hate crime hoax.

Remember that the next time CNN's Jim Acosta throws a hissy fit and whines, "We are real news, Mr. President," or the next time you see one of those low-rate "Facts First" videos with the apples and bananas (yes, CNN does think you're so retarded that you need a first-grade level illustration), or the next time you're channel surfing and you stumble across Brian Stelter's show, *Reliable Sources*, which is named as though he's trying to convince himself that he's not full of shit.

In 2011, a lesbian couple in Colorado, Aimee Whitchurch and Christel Conklin, reported to police that their rented condominium had been vandalized with anti-gay graffiti. They said that the words "Kill the Gay" were spray painted on their garage, and that a noose was left on their doorstep.

The Anti-Defamation League went to bat for the couple.

"All Coloradoans deserve to feel safe in their homes. Hate crimes threaten the victims' safety and send a message that not all are welcomed and protected," said the ADL's Scott L. Levin at the time.

This is where we live," Whitchurch said. "We should feel safe. I'm afraid to walk outside my place now."[153]

Before all the facts were settled, the local media shamed the homeowner's association into issuing an apology to the couple, and for covering the graffiti with white paint, which apparently clashed with the couple's brown garage. Don't get me wrong, HOA's should be outlawed for the simple fact that they make annoying and arbitrary rules, a pet peeve of mine. But *come on.* They had nothing to do with the alleged hate crime. Why on earth would it matter that they didn't apologize?

The homeowner's association was vindicated for their lack of apology when the FBI became involved in the investigation. The feds tested the couple's hands for spray paint residue, and asked them to take a lie detector test, which they declined to do. It was then determined that they had committed the "hate crime" against themselves. As it turned out, they had a prior beef with the homeowner's association, and played the media like a fiddle in trying to make the HOA look like schmucks. The press—non-curious and looking for a juicy story—ran with the couple's fake story of victimization.[154]

Both women were eventually charged with two counts of criminal mischief and two counts of filing false reports. The homeowner's association should have demanded an apology from the local media.

Not all hate crime hoaxes are created equal. Some include an attempt to bilk money out of innocent victims who want to support the alleged victim. That is exactly what happened in the case of Julie Baker, a Baltimore resident who claimed that an anonymous neighbor left her a nasty note, telling her that her yard had become "relentlessly gay."

"Your yard is becoming Relentlessly Gay! Myself and Others in the neighborhood ask that you Tone it Down. This is a Christian area and there are Children. Keep it up and I will be forced to call the police on You! Your kind need to have Respect for GOD," the note said, according to Baker.[155]

It was signed "A Concerned Neighbor."

Baker then set up a GoFundMe account in an attempt to profit off of the alleged hate crime.

Cosmopolitan gushed over the way Baker handled the situation in an article titled "Woman who was told her garden is 'relentlessly gay' responds in the BEST way."[156] *Cosmo* wrote:

> So now, Julie has decided to do the only sensible thing - make her garden "even more 'relentlessly gay'[sic], setting up a GoFundMe page to make some much-needed alterations.
>
> "Needless to say... I need more rainbows... Many, many more rainbows."
>
> "So, I am starting this fundraiser so I can work to make my Home even more 'relentlessly gay'. If we go high enough, I will see if I can get a Rainbow Roof! Because my invisible relentlessly gay rainbow dragon should live up there in style!
>
> "Put simply, I am a widow and the mother of four children, my youngest in high school and I WILL NOT relent to hatred. Instead, I will battle it with whimsy and beauty and laughter and love, wrapped around my home, yard and family!!! Thanks for your relentlessly gay support!"

The publication even linked to Baker's GoFundMe to assist in her fundraising efforts.

When curious internet investigators began to question Baker's story, noting that the distinctive capitalization and punctuation style of the alleged note matched that of several social media posts made by Baker, the story began to fall apart. Authorities were notified, and Baker refused to produce the actual note that she claimed was left at her home. All of this after she raised $43,000, thanks to gullible media outlets like *Cosmopolitan*. Baker disabled the fundraising page six days after she initiated it, and assured that she would not withdraw any of the funds until the note could be authenticated. But the note was never authenticated, because it was not authentic.

Baker returned the money and faded into the background after her fifteen minutes of fame were up. She was not charged with a crime for attempted grift.

The king of all hate crime hoaxes in recent memory occurred only days before the 2016 presidential election, and the press worked overtime trying to use the hoax to advance the idea that a Trump presidency would inevitably lead to race war. Someone ought to tell media that America has been in the midst of an escalating race war since former anchor Sally Kohn and her gang at CNN promulgated the bogus "Hands Up, Don't Shoot" narrative on live television after the shooting of Michael Brown by a Ferguson, Missouri police officer in 2014.[157] One could argue that "Hands Up, Don't Shoot" was the most blatant lie ever told by the press, as forensic evidence proved that Brown charged the officer and attempted to grab his gun before being shot,[158] and the racial animosity in this country has only mounted since the Ferguson ordeal.

In early November 2016, Hopewell Missionary Baptist Church in Greenville, Mississippi was torched and nearly burned to the ground. On the side of the church, in gigantic white letters, the words "Vote Trump" were spray-painted. Due to the timing of the attack, the fact that the church was historically black, and the message spray-painted on the church, it was perhaps the most politically poignant hate crime hoax in history.

The Atlantic was all-too-happy to run a headline that read "A Black Church Was Burned in the Name of Trump"[159] well before any of the facts had been established. They followed the headline up by claiming that no one knew anything about the arson, except that it was caused by Trump, of course!

"In this case, though, someone left a calling card about politics. It's not yet clear who set the fire, if anyone set it; whether the person who set the fire is the same person who wrote the graffiti; or why, if the fire was intentional, Hopewell M.B. Church was the target. One thing is clear, though: At some point, someone decided to attach the name of Trump to a burned black church," the article read.

NBC made sure that the *lede* of their story on the incident was a quote from the town's mayor, Errick Simmons, who called it "an attack on the black community."

"It appears to be a race crime. It happened in the '50s. It happened in the '60s. It shouldn't happen in 2016," Simmons said.[160]

The news network even embedded a Tweet from then-candidate Hillary Clinton, who used the arson to score political points.

"The perpetrators who set the Hopewell M.B. Church in MS on fire must be brought to justice. This kind of hate has no place in America," Clinton Tweeted.[161] At least the Tweet appeared sincere, unlike her other embarrassing attempts to connect with black voters on the campaign trail, like claiming that she kept hot sauce in her purse at all times.[162]

PBS ran a story in which it quoted J. Blair Reeves Jr., a community member who started a fundraiser to rebuild the church and who tacitly blamed Trump for the fire.

"The animus of this election cycle combined with the potent racial history of burning black churches as a political symbol makes this event something we must not ignore," he said.[163]

The Telegraph ran nearly the same script but with different characters, quoting Kristen Clarke, president and executive director of the Lawyers' Committee for Civil Rights Under Law, who said "The toxic rhetoric of this election cycle continues to cast a dark cloud over this election cycle."[164]

The Daily Beast ran a column called "A Burned Down Black Church Shows President Trump Won't Condemn His Own Terrorists."[165] The columnist, Justin Glawe, scorched Trump for not issuing a personal statement regarding the arson, while lauding Clinton for typing a hundred characters into a cell phone app:

> *Hillary Clinton immediately took to Twitter to condemn the act, saying, "This kind of hate has no place in America." It was signed "H" to show it was from Clinton herself. But when it came to the burning of a black church in his own name, Trump's little fingers didn't touch his favorite means of reaching millions of supporters, Twitter. Instead, his campaign issued a boilerplate statement. So these are stakes of this election: a*

potential president who would not even condemn in his own words terrorism done in his own name.

But after all of the leftist media outrage, the perpetrator of the arson turned out to be a black male and a parishioner of the church. Andrew McClinton, a forty-five-year-old resident of the town and previous felon, was arrested six weeks later and charged with the arson. Many of the aforementioned media outlets updated their stories with short blurbs about the arrest. None apologized for falsely blaming Trump.

The press makes millions of dollars in revenue from website traffic earned from stories like the ones detailed here. Millions of Americans have bought into the fabricated narrative that Trump's America is racist, dark, and evil. It is in the interest of the press—and its financial bottom line—to continue to publish such stories casting Republicans in a negative light, even if the facts of each alleged hate crime have not been established at the time of publication. What should Americans call a press that is contributing to a potential race war? Some might call them the enemy.

CHAPTER 7

MEDIA VIOLENCE

When a violent revolution breaks out in the streets of America, the mainstream news media will be to blame. Not only do they actively sow discord among political factions in the name of ratings and profit, but for years they have been excusing, promoting, and apologizing for leftist mob violence, harassment, and incivility towards Republicans. It is now par for the course for talking heads in cable news to run cover for leftists while leftists run wild in the streets.

A group called "Smash Racism" published the home address of Fox News host Tucker Carlson in November 2018, which led to a horde of masked Antifa radicals showing up at his home, marching on his lawn, ringing his doorbell, and threatening his family.[166]

"We know where you sleep at night," the group yelled menacingly, adding that Carlson and his family should "leave town" and warning them that they "were not safe." A woman could also be heard saying that she wanted to "pipe bomb" Carlson's home.

Carlson's wife reportedly locked herself in the pantry of their home, expecting the group to break down their front door, which is nearly what ended up happening. One of the crazed psychopaths physically threw himself against the door, leaving a crack in it.[167] The choice of Carlson as a target was purely political. Anyone who advocates for sane immigration policy, which Tucker does frequently on his show, is labeled as a "white nationalist" or a "racist" by the left-wing press. When sentiment then boils over into the streets, Carlson's wife ends up hiding in the pantry of their home, terrified and hoping that she doesn't meet her demise at the hands of radical leftists.

The textbook definition of terrorism is "the unlawful use of violence and intimidation, especially against civilians, in the pursuit of political aims."[168]

Antifa's romp on Carslon's lawn meets that definition. But you can bet that the mainstream press neglected to report from that angle.

Far-left *Vox*'s co-founder Matt Yglesias handled the situation with the least tact, actively defending the group's actions. He said that he had "no empathy" for Carlson's family, and that "the idea behind terrorizing [Carlson's] family...is to make them feel some of the fear that the victims of MAGA-inspired violence feel thanks to the non-stop racial incitement coming from Tucker, Trump, etc."[169] This is a textbook example about how mainstream media's mostly tacit—but sometimes overt—endorsement of left-wing violence has real ramifications outside the news studio.

Neither Trump nor Tucker have ever physically aggressed anyone, and differences in policy beliefs on immigration are neither racist, nor justification for terrorizing Carlson's family. These facts are lost on the revered members of the mainstream press, who hate Republicans and would absolutely have us lined up against a wall and shot, if only it were socially acceptable. Later during the same evening, Yglesias deleted every single Tweet from his Twitter timeline and started anew.

Frequent CNN and MSNBC guest Soledad O'Brien also justified the attack on Twitter because, in her view, Carlson is a "racist."[170]

"Yes well when you're a racist, saying what you think might end up ousting you from your job. So yes, people will bash you when you take the white supremacist position that diversity is not a strength. Don't be a racist," she said.

Aside from the fact that Carlson is demonstrably *not* a racist, are these really the guidelines that we want to set for our society? Should someone like O'Brien's subjective opinion on whether another person is "racist" serve as a rationale for violence? The political left has a sincerely held belief that every person who supports President Trump—all 63 million of their fellow Americans—is racist. By O'Brien's logic, all of them would be justified targets of leftist terrorism. Is that the path that we're headed down? These are real questions that the media needs to consider before they thrust this nation into a civil war.

The incident at Carlson's was the type that has become all-too-common from the far left, which does not understand the difference between law-breaking and legitimate, First Amendment protected protest. Neither, apparently, does the press, which normalizes that type of behavior regularly.

Take CNN's Chris Cuomo, for example, anchor of "Cuomo Primetime."

In August 2018, Cuomo ran a segment on his show where the chyron on the bottom of the screen read "No Moral Equivalency Between Nazis & Antifa." In the segment, he defended Antifa thugs physically battering pro-Trump demonstrators in Washington, D.C.[171] Even journalists covering the event were attacked by the "anti-fascists." That made no difference to Cuomo. The mainstream media only cares about the "free press" when they are attacking Trump for rightfully calling them the enemy of the people. Selective outrage is a hallmark of left-wing politics.

"People who show up to fight against bigots are not to be judged the same as the bigots even if they do resort to the same kinds of petty violence," Cuomo said.

The Trump supporters at the rally had not resorted to any violence. Apparently, perceived bigotry is indeed justification for physical violence at CNN.

Worse still, to the pea-brained political left, conditioned like Pavlov's dogs by the very same mainstream press, the definition of "Nazi" is "anyone who disagrees with me," just like the definition of "racist" is "anyone who supports Donald Trump." Thus, there will *always* be a rationale for violence according to the political left. The very act of Republican existence is enough for leftists to excuse violence against them.

Cable news peddles such garbage for the same reason it peddles all of its other garbage. Violence sells advertisements. Why purchase an HBO subscription when Cuomo and company will pipe a violent action thriller into your living room every night? Coincidentally (or perhaps not), HBO's parent company is WarnerMedia, which owns TBS. TBS owns CNN. That sounds like a bad SAT question, but just know that CNN and HBO are owned by the same people.

Who are all these supposed "Nazis" anyway? All Republicans ever wanted were closed borders and sensible legal immigration policies. But to the fine folks at CNN/WarnerMedia/HBO/TBS, that is equivalent to the genocide of six million Jews.

Let's don our thinking caps for a second. Cuomo is a half-wit. That much is settled. But even he is not stupid enough to actually believe that Republicans and German Nazis exist on the same moral plane. That means that he is knowingly lying when he reports from this angle. He is pushing the "Nazi" narrative for one reason. It pays the bills. So by all means, get out there and punch some of those Republican "Nazis." And don't even worry about it, because when you do punch a "Nazi," Cuomo will cover for you.

Cuomo's colleague Don Lemon also defended the Antifa violence from the same riot. The two take their notes from the same corporate media executives, after all. Original thought is strictly disallowed at CNN. By the way, if anyone dubbed "Nazi" or "racist" deserves a beat down, which appears to be the argument, then CNN's Lemon should be on the short list considering his well-documented history of anti-white racism. Maybe Cuomo or O'Brien could address that with him sometime.

"It says it right in the name: Antifa. Anti-fascism, which is what they were there (in Charlottesville) fighting," Lemon said on his show in defense of Antifa.[172]

Lemon's argument boils down to *"res ipsa loquitur,* bitches!" The name of the group obviously speaks for itself! And since nothing has ever been misnamed, that argument makes total sense! Except how will Lemon explain that strawberries, bayberries, blackberries, and raspberries are not actually berries? Or that the French Horn originated in Germany? Or that the "funny bone" is not actually a bone? Or that neither flying foxes nor flying squirrels actually fly? What if I get "tennis elbow" from playing racquetball? Does that mean tennis is actually racquetball? What if I change my name to King Tut? Will Lemon make the case that I'm the famous pharaoh of the 18th Egyptian dynasty? "But Don...*it says it right in my name.*"

Remember, this is the same elitist press that constantly derides Middle American Trump supporters as intellectually inferior. Somehow, the "intellectually inferior" have managed to figure out that, despite its name, Antifa is violently suppressing the free exchange of ideas—precisely what fascists do—and that they're the only political group in America behaving in such a manner. This, while the laggards in the press sit behind their desks drooling. It's almost like Antifa is misnamed after all!

"Listen, no organization's perfect," Lemon continued. "There was some violence. No one condones violence, but there were different reasons for Antifa and for these neo-Nazis to be there. One, racists, fascists, the other group, fighting racist fascists. There is a distinction there."

In other words, no one condones violence unless it's violence against people that CNN doesn't like. In that case, CNN condones violence. Just remember that *no one condones violence.*

Lemon and Cuomo teamed up to tell each other how correct they were when it comes to supporting Antifa terrorism after

Sen. Ted Cruz (R-TX) and his wife Heidi were chased out of a Washington, D.C. restaurant over Cruz's support for Supreme Court Justice Brett Kavanaugh in September 2018.[173]

Kavanaugh, you might remember, was accused of sexual misconduct just before his confirmation to the nation's highest court. The accusations were completely unprovable, and Democrats knew that—but they proceeded to tarnish a good man's name because he is a conservative. The group harassing Cruz was "Smash Racism," the same one that tried to break down Tucker Carlson's front door. The group accompanied the video of Cruz's harassment with a message saying "You are not safe. We will find you. We will expose you. We will take from you the peace you have taken from so many others."[174]

Of the harassment inside a private establishment, Lemon said the following:

> *"It's a tough one, Chris. Because, one, it's survivors, right? Of sexual abuse. I'm one. As a person of color, I know that, especially during the Civil Rights movement, and now, sometimes the only agency you have is to protest, and to get in someone's face. You don't have any power when it comes to government and in society. I don't like it, but it is one reason I'm not a public official, that I'm not running for office. In a way, I think it goes with the territory. I don't like that they were blocking his wife, but, that's what he signed up for. And as a strict Constitutionalist, which Ted Cruz is, he knows that it's protected under the First Amendment. Again, I don't like it, I wouldn't want it to happen to me, I don't like it*

happening to his wife. But he...that's what he signed up
for. That's part of the deal."[175]

For the record, there is no Constitutional right to harass someone inside a restaurant. Lemon is clearly reaching on the "peaceably assemble" portion of the First Amendment.

The restaurant was so thrilled with the "peaceful protesting" that they hired armed security guards shortly thereafter, just in case any more peace broke out and they needed to deal with it accordingly.[176]

Shortly after a sixteen-year-old and his friends were assaulted by a thirty-year-old loser in a San Antonio, Texas Whataburger restaurant, then-CNN analyst and Temple University professor Marc Lamont Hill defended the actions of the assailant. Kino Jimenez stole the teenager's MAGA hat inside the restaurant and threw a drink in the teen's face.[177]

"I actually don't advocate throwing drinks on people. Not at all. But yes, I think MAGA hats (deliberately) reflect a movement that conjures racism, homophobia, xenophobia, etc. So yes, it's a little harder to feel sympathy when someone gets Coca Cola thrown on him," Hill said on Twitter.[178]

To be perfectly clear, Hill doesn't "advocate throwing drinks on people" unless those people are wearing a hat with a specific message that he deems to be racist. In that case, it's open season for violence.

Months later, Hill proved that he absolutely *does not* justify political violence by justifying Palestinian political violence during a speech at the United Nations.

"Contrary to western mythology, black resistance to American apartheid did not come purely through Gandhi and nonviolence," he said. "Rather, slave revolts and self-defense and tactics otherwise divergent from Dr. King or Mahatma Gandhi were equally important to preserving safety and attaining freedom."[179]

Those comments, which were literal calls for violence against Israel, did not turn any heads because the mainstream press has desensitized Americans to political violence. Only with his next comments did Hill get controversial. He said that justice for Palestinians requires a "free Palestine from the river to the sea." That line is a reference to the total destruction of Israel, which would necessarily require the genocide of all Israeli people. It is commonly used by Jew-hating terrorist groups like Hamas, who are actively working on invading Israel and genociding its Jewish inhabitants. (In the immortal words of Don Lemon: "Listen, no organization is perfect.")

Apparently, this is where the press draws the line. Hill was fired from CNN for his comments. Don't worry, though. He's still employed by Temple University, where he will continue to mold the minds of American youth.

Occasionally, CNN gets out of the studio and joins in harassment and violence against Republicans. In February 2018, Americans learned that some Russian plants created Facebook events to rally people in the streets before the 2016 elections. Those targeted were from all political backgrounds, including Black Lives Matter, Occupy Wall Street, and Bernie Sanders supporters, which CNN conveniently buried in the last paragraph of a long article titled "The unwitting: The

Trump supporters used by Russia."[180] As if the article weren't bad enough, CNN doxed a Facebook grandma who allegedly ran the page used by those evil Russians to coordinate a pro-Trump event. They published her name in the article, and a video of reporter Drew Griffin harassing her on her front lawn in a Twitter post that linked to the article.[181] The doxing led to the woman receiving death threats and thousands of harassing comments online.[182]

> *"You disgusting old communist pig. Traitor!!!" one Facebook user wrote to the woman.*

> *"You're just gonna have to delete your account, you treasonous hillbilly," another said.*

> *"[S]tay in Florida, come to NY and I'll kick your Russian bot ass," said another.*

All in a day's work over at CNN. They did not go through the trouble of doxing anyone from the left-wing organizations "duped" by Russians. In any case, the alleged duping was obviously inconsequential to the election results.

When the *Cable News Network* is not actively doxing people, it is threatening others with such behavior. Reporter Andrew Kaczynski (no relation to Unabomber, Ted, but more dangerous) tracked down the personal details of a Reddit user called "HanAssholeSolo," who made a .gif image of Trump body-slamming CNN in a wrestling wring.[183] Kaczynski, who goes by "KFile," identified the man behind the "HanAssholeSolo" by using information that "HanAssholeSolo" posted on Reddit. He was then able to determine key biographical details, find the man's name using a Facebook search, and ultimately corroborate details HanAssholeSolo had made available on Reddit.

All of this over an image that rubbed Kaczynski the wrong way. He was so grossly offended by the image that he publicly bragged about learning the man's personal information and forced him to apologize on Reddit for fear of doxing by CNN. Then he bragged about strong arming the anonymous Reddit user in an article that he proudly wrote about himself in the third person:

> Now the user is apologizing, writing in a lengthy post on Reddit that he does not advocate violence against the press and expressing remorse there and in an interview with CNN for other posts he made that were racist and anti-Semitic.... On Monday, KFile attempted to contact the man by email and phone but he did not respond. On Tuesday, "HanA**holeSolo" posted his apology on the subreddit /The_Donald and deleted all of his other posts.

It was a Pulitzer Prize worthy win for CNN. Truly impressive sleuthing. They managed to take down an anonymous internet troll! What petty, pathetic little twerps they are.

In another incident of CNN inciting and supporting violence, harassment, and incivility towards Trump and Republicans, late CNN host Anthony Bourdain "joked" about poisoning Trump. Around the time that Trump was making peace with

North Korea and averting nuclear war, Bourdain, former host of CNN's *Parts Unknown,* was asked by TMZ what he would serve for dinner, given the opportunity to cook for Kim and Trump.

"Hemlock," Bourdain responded.[184]

Hemlock is a poison that was used as an execution method in ancient times.

Shortly before Trump's inauguration, CNN ran an entire segment with a chyron that read "Disaster Could Put Obama Cabinet Member in Oval Office."[185] The theme of the segment, as you might have gathered, was what would have happened if Trump and Vice President-Elect Mike Pence had been assassinated during the inauguration proceedings. The segment had a hopeful tone.

> *Tonight, due to a quirk in America's rules for succession, questions remain about just who would be in charge if an attack hit the incoming president, vice president, and Congressional leaders just as the transfer of power is underway.... According to the Constitution, if the president or vice president are killed or incapacitated, next in line is the House Speaker, then the president pro-tempore of the Senate. But what if something happened to them at the inauguration, too? After that, it goes down the list of cabinet secretaries, starting with Secretary of State. On the day of inauguration, as a precaution, a cabinet secretary called the "designated presidential successor," will not attend the inauguration, ready to step in if something happens.*

CNN then assured its audience that that cabinet member would be a member of the Obama administration, as Trump's cabinet would not have been confirmed at that point. If you're curious, based on CNN's scenario, Tom Shannon, the Undersecretary for Political Affairs, would have gotten the nod had CNN's fantasy become reality. Shannon is altogether unremarkable in terms of presidential candidates. The peak of his political career was his service as United States Ambassador to Brazil.[186]

CNN even ran a full profile piece on a man who attempted to rush the stage at a Trump campaign rally in March 2016. They turned this guy into a hero—a regular luminary for all the crazies who might want to physically attack Trump.[187]

When Thomas DiMassimo tried to rush Donald Trump's stage in Ohio over the weekend, he had a clear goal in mind.

He wanted to send a message.

"I was thinking that I could get up on stage and take his podium away from him and take his mic away from him and send a message to all people out in the country who wouldn't consider themselves racist, who wouldn't consider themselves approving of what type of violence Donald Trump is allowing in his rallies, and send them a message that we can be strong, that we can find our strength and we can stand up against Donald Trump and against this new wave he's ushering in of truly just violent white supremacist ideas," DiMassimo told CNN.

"I was thinking that Donald Trump is a bully, and he is nothing more than that. He is somebody who is just saying a lot of bold things, he's making bold claims. But I can see right through that and I can see that he's truly just a coward. And he's opportunistic and he's willing to destroy this country for power for himself," DiMassimo said.

DiMassimo never made it to the stage. He was flattened by Secret Service before he even got close. After being peeled off the floor, he was arrested and charged with disorderly conduct and inducing panic. Not to worry, though. CNN reported that their fearless leader DiMassimo remained "unafraid" despite his stonewalling.

Lest you were thinking CNN is the only mainstream press shop that advocates for violence on a regular basis, there are plenty of other examples from plenty of other corporate news outlets.

Take MSNBC's "counter-terrorism analyst" Malcolm Nance, for example, who called for ISIS to bomb the Trump Tower in Istanbul, Turkey.

"This is my nominee for the first suicide bombing of a Trump property," Nance said in a now-deleted Tweet, linking to a story about the Trump Tower in Turkey.[188]

MSNBC completely ignored the incident, and Nance never apologized. After one of its employees called for ISIS, America's literal enemy, to bomb one of Trump's properties, the network is still scratching its collective head trying to figure out why Trump might call them the enemy of the American people.

Former congressional spokesman Kurt Bardella joined MSNBC's resident homophobe Joy-Ann Reid on a panel in March 2018, where they hoped that Second Amendment supporting Republicans would simply "die off."[189]

Reid hypothesized that conservative media will eventually run out of viewers, to which Bardella responded, "I think there is some credence to the idea that, at some point, just the process of evolution, some of these viewers, they are going to thankfully die off, and that'll be the end of that."

We've finally found a way to placate the left-wing press. Simply die, and they'll be happy.

NBC's Chuck Todd minced no words when he suggested a solution to dealing with right-wing "fascists."

"Historically, fascism has only been defeated with violence," Todd, host of *Meet the Press,* said in an interview with Dartmouth professor Mark Bray in 2017.[190]

Bray is the author of *Antifa: The Anti-Fascist Handbook.* The context of Todd's interview with Bray was how to combat "white supremacists" and "fascists," defined as "Trump supporters." It is utterly deranged to argue that all 63 million people who voted for Trump, and others who support him but may not have voted for him, are white supremacists, fascists, or Nazis. But press traffics in utter derangement, so that won't stop hacks like Todd.

"Self-defense is important," Bray said. "I think the notion that people are seeing the self-defense as counterproductive is not entirely true, and I think self-defense is important. Fascism shows that it is violence incarnate. It will come out. It is violence, and we have to defend ourselves."

But Antifa, emboldened by the press which gladly platforms clowns like Bray, is not acting in self-defense. By and large, they are the aggressors. Trump supporters cannot assemble in public to support the president anymore without being assailed by violent leftists. There are enough examples of Antifa violence against Republicans to write an entire book on that subject alone. But we don't have time for that here, so back to our friendly mainstream media it is.

When the press is not defending violent radicals in the streets or inciting violence against Republicans, it is usually fantasizing about Trump's death.

The New York Times published a Trump assassination fantasy in an article called "Five Novelists Imagine Trump's Next Chapter"[191] in October 2018. The article was comprised of the work of "five fiction writers," which is usually just called *The New York Times* Sunday Edition. Here is author Zoë Sharp's depiction of how it ends for Trump, as published in the *Times*:

The Russian waited until they were a few steps past before he drew the gun. He sighted on the center of the president's back, and squeezed the trigger.

The Makarov misfired.

The Secret Service agent at the president's shoulder heard the click, spun into a crouch. He registered the scene instantly, drawing his own weapon with razor-edge reflexes.

The Russian tasted failure. He closed his eyes and waited to pay the cost.

It did not come.

He opened his eyes. The Secret Service agent stood before him, presenting his Glock, butt first.

"Here," the agent said politely. "Use mine...."

The same paper published an opinion in July 2018 from its editorial board encouraging Democrats to resort to violence in order to halt the confirmation of Supreme Court Justice Brett Kavanaugh, given that his confirmation would lead to a 5-4 conservative-leaning majority on the Court.[192]

"This is all the more reason for Democrats and progressives to take a page from 'The Godfather' and go to the mattresses on this issue," the editorial said. "Because this battle is about more than a single seat on the nation's highest court."

"Go to the mattresses" is a euphemism for starting a gang war. In total, there are forty-two murders in "The Godfather" trilogy,[193] most of them brutal. Here are the precise types of violence against Republicans explicitly endorsed by the *Times* with its "Godfather" quip: shooting, wrist slitting, poisoning, smothering to suffocation, garroting, and disemboweling.

During the same month, comedienne turned political pundit Rosie O'Donnell called on the military to overthrow Trump during a guest spot on MSNBC.[194]

"[And] I want to send the military to the White House to get him," she told Chris Wallace, making the panel giddy.

In July 2018, *The New Yorker* published a cover which depicted Trump falling flat on his face at the bottom of an escalator, which prompted a rare Tweet from center-right news aggregator Matt Drudge.[195]

"The Left's continued fetish for Trump's physical harm/death is stunning," Drudge said.

The cover illustrator, Barry Blitt, laughed it off as a harmless joke.

"Well, I can tell you that outrage makes for easier humor than agreement does—but, then again, agreement can be pretty hilarious," he said.[196]

More brazenly, *HuffPost* was forced to retract a June 2017 piece wherein contributor Jason Fuller called for the "ultimate punishment" of Trump.[197]

"Trump must be prosecuted - if convicted in a court of law - executed," Fuller said. He referred to execution and "ultimate punishment" twice each in the piece. He also included others on his hit list who were "assisting in [Trump's] agenda." Listed were Senate Majority Leader Mitch McConnell (R-KY) and Stephen K. Bannon, former White House Chief Strategist.

The list of instances of deranged left-wing talking heads and writers blabbering on in defense of violence, harassment, and terrorism against Trump supporters goes on and on (and on, and on, and on). The media simply cannot help themselves. They are bursting at the seams with Trump hatred, and now more frequently than ever they are letting that hatred shine through.

It is a dangerous time in America when media influencers actively condone that type of behavior against half of the population. For this alone, they could rightfully be labeled as enemies of the people. Unfortunately, there is more to the story.

CHAPTER 8

FACT-CHECKING THE FACT-CHECKERS

A while back, I wrote a story which factually stated that forensic experts had debunked the mainstream press's conspiracy theory about Press Secretary Sarah Huckabee Sanders sharing a "manipulated" video of Jim Acosta assaulting a White House intern during a press briefing.[198]

You might remember the incident. Acosta was arguing with Trump as he so often and annoyingly does, and in order to keep possession of the microphone, he karate chopped a young female intern who was instructed by Trump to take it away. For this, his White House press credentials were revoked.

Immediately after the revocation, the corporate press went to work telling Americans that they did not, in fact, see exactly what they saw. Most outlets claimed that Acosta never touched the woman, and the video was manipulated to make it appear as such, a message that was echoed by the arbiters of internet truth at *Snopes*.[199]

After finding out that the video shared by Sanders was legitimate, as proven by forensic experts, I contacted *Snopes'* founder David Mikkelson to ask why his site, which is responsible for deciding what is true and what is false on the internet in its official capacity as a "fact-checker," would spread misinformation. I also asked whether they would retract their story, and most importantly whether they would "fact-check" all of the mainstream press outlets who made false claims that the video was doctored. Mikkelson took offense to my question (how could anyone question the ordained truth ministers at Snopes?), and responded with an email that was, in short, pure bullshit.

A few days later, White House Counsel Kellyanne Conway, in a discussion with Fox News' Chris Wallace, agreed with Wallace that the video in question was actually "sped up."[200] I then received a follow-up email from Mikkelson asking if I would retract *my* story, given what Conway said on air. It was precisely then that I discovered the barometer of truth for the esteemed "fact-checkers" of the internet: the apparently infallible opinions of Kellyanne Conway.

My story said that *forensic experts* who studied the video decided that it was not manipulated. That was a factual story, based on quotes from real forensic experts. Mikkelson wanted me to retract it because Kellyanne Conway, who is *not a forensic expert*, said otherwise. This was a prima facie case of Snopes foolishness.

Alas, I don't make the rules. Mikkelson is charged with that task. It's his world. We newsies are just living in it. So now, whenever I have a question of fact whilst writing an article, I simply dial up Kellyanne and ask her what she thinks. That way, I can thumb my nose at that goofball Mikkelson and tell him to kick rocks if his organization ever questions the veracity of one of my stories.

For the record, I did not retract the story, and tellingly, he never made a move after my retraction refusal. He was simply trying to strong-arm me into backing off my reporting because he is a partner of Facebook, making him an ancillary member of the left-wing Palo Alto Mafia, which has made it very clear that the internet is leftist turf. Mikkelson's retraction request was the media version of threatening to break my knee caps if I didn't pay my respects to the Mafiosi at Snopes.

You see, the "fact-checkers" in the press are not actually interested in the truth, sort of like the rest of the press. They are simply left-wing hatchet shops used to bully conservative news sites and protect the mainstream press at all costs under the guise of being "impartial." The sole purpose for the existence of sites like Snopes and *PolitiFact* is to make sure that no other narrative than the one deemed appropriate by the mainstream press is taken seriously. They are the most dishonest group of scumbags ever to grace the internet with their presence. They are worse than the mainstream press in that they actively suppress anything that is not mainstream press. Pro-Trump news is not allowed to exist in the world of the "fact-checkers," because that might challenge the ever-so-intellectual narrative spewed by the corporate media that the orange man in the Oval Office is *literally Hitler*, and that he's bound to kill us all one way or another. The "fact-checkers" are the anti-media. They— not President Trump—stand for suppression of the free press and the First Amendment, and against the American people. Some might even call them the enemy.

And they have a *ton* of power. When Snopes calls Kellyanne Conway to confirm whether a story is true, and Kellyanne says it's not, they have the ability to send a notification to everyone on Facebook who shared the story, telling the Facebook user that the story has been "disputed" by Snopes. The site actually received $100,000 from the left-wingers at Facebook as part of their "fact-checking" partnership.[201] It turns out there's a nice chunk of change involved in "fact-checking" between such partnerships and, of course, selling advertisements. *PolitiFact* has the same ability as Snopes to flag "false" stories. So does the Associated Press, who recently decided to get in on the fact-checking con. Rumor has it that each refuted story results in a "strike," and that after a certain amount of "strikes," Zuckerberg's minions will nuke the news organization's page completely. Of this I am not positive, and I could not get ahold of Kellyanne—so perhaps if Mikkelson reads this he can set the record straight.

Fact-checkers could actually be useful on the web, if they indeed checked facts. But I'm talking about real, provable, quantifiably measurable facts. The current operations involve parsing words, making subjective assessments about what a site's claim actually means, and splitting hairs in order to sow doubt about the veracity of any story not published by a website with an accompanying cable news network.

For an example of how the fact-checkers employ weasel-wording to mislead their audience, look no further than the story of the sea turtle. The question that Snopes sought to clarify was whether "President Donald Trump canceled federal protections for whales and sea turtles."[202]

"The decision was not made by Donald Trump himself, nor did it overturn or cancel several other existing protections for marine mammals both off the West Coast and nationwide," the site said.

So the answer, in plain English, is no—Donald Trump did not cancel federal protections for sea turtles. But Snopes rated the claim as a "mixture" of truth and falsehood.

According to the illustrious "fact-checkers," the National Marine Fisheries Service "decided not to implement a proposal that would have shut down one particular fishery off the coast of California if a certain number of protected marine mammals were entangled in fishing nets and killed."

Some federal agency was faced with the question of whether they would shut down this single fishery in the event that a certain number of whales and sea turtles were caught in fishing nets and killed. Apparently, that agency answered the question in the negative.

Let's do some math here. The National Marine Fisheries Service does not equal Donald Trump. In fact, I'd wager that if you asked Trump to name one person employed by the National Marine Fisheries Service, he would ask, "What the hell is that, and why are we wasting money on it?" Back to the math. Refusing to implement a plan does not equal canceling a plan. The plan must first be implemented before it can be canceled. Neither Trump, nor the Fisheries Service, canceled anything. Thus, the answer to Snopes' question of whether "President Donald Trump canceled federal protections for whales and sea turtles" is no. It is unequivocally "no." It is the opposite of "yes." It is not "yes" and "no." It is plainly, flatly, simply "no."

I asked Mikkelson why he rated the claim as a "mixture" when anyone with a pulse would recognize that the answer is "no."

"We know from long experience that when readers pose policy questions along the lines of "Did President [XXX] set/change this policy?" they are generally using the president's name as a metonym for the current government/administration," Mikkelson said. "Therefore, we have to address the broader question in order to avoid being misleading."[203]

In that answer to my question, Mikkelson revealed the real "fact-checking" formula. Snopes is not simply answering questions posed by readers. They are subjectively assessing the meaning of the questions asked by readers before they answer them, rather than taking the questions at face value. This subjective analysis, Mikkelson claims, is done in an effort to "avoid being misleading." But in itself, that process is misleading. Who is Mikkelson to decide what you meant by your question? Not to mention, he didn't even run the question by Kellyanne Conway! In light of that, can we really trust the answer?

For safe measure, Mikkelson added that Snopes was not afraid to disprove negative rumors about Trump, and that his site often does so.

Are you starting to understand how this game is played? If so, don't worry. It gets worse.

When Rep. Eric Swalwell (D-CA) responded to a defiant gun rights activist on Twitter who warned him that gun confiscation would lead to a civil war, Swalwell quipped that it would be a "short war" because "the government has nukes."[204] Immediately, the right-leaning independent press, including this author, jumped all over the story. After all, it's not every day that a U.S. Congressman intimates at dropping the most powerful weaponry in the history of man onto the collective heads of American citizens. And that is exactly how most of us reported it—as an intimation. We weren't running around willy-nilly strapping on our high school football helmets, pulling fire alarms, and diving under our desks preparing for the big blast. The suggestion alone of nuking the citizenry by such a high-level government official is a huge story in itself. We did not need to embellish it, or pretend that Swalwell had his finger on the launch button, for the story to be a jaw dropper.

But Snopes could not let our factual stories go unchallenged, so they did what Snopes does. They ran a headline that read "Did Democrat Rep. Eric Swalwell 'Suggest Nuking' Gun Owners Who Resist Confiscation?"[8] The site concluded that our claims in the media were a "mixture" of truth and falsehood. What was false about our reporting on exactly what the Congressman said, verbatim? Well, according to Snopes, Swalwell was just kidding. In other words, Swalwell didn't mean what he said, so the right-wing press is clearly lying!

"Swalwell quickly insisted that his reference to the government's possession of nuclear weapons was intended as no more than a joke and emphasized that he was not warning gun owners about such a response to their (hypothetical) resistance to gun confiscation," the site explained.

Apparently, the "just kidding" defense is now applicable at the leisure of any idiot Congressman who makes an ass out of himself on Twitter.

Even if he was kidding, what is it about the presence of a joke that negates the suggestion? It is possible—indeed common—to joke and make a suggestion at the same time. Unless you dwell in the annals of the left-wing media, shilling to protect boyish Congressmen in order to make a few bucks. Snopes' "logic" leaves much to be desired.

Swalwell: "The sky is red."

Snopes: "We rate that claim as 'false.'"

Swalwell: "Just kidding!"

Snopes: "Never mind, he was just kidding. The sky must be red!"

Worst of all, Swalwell, being the colossal moron that he is, shared the link to the Snopes article on Twitter, saying that it "DEBUNKED" (he used all caps) all of those stories that were written about his nuke comments.[205] Unfortunately for Swalwell, the Twittersphere has Snopes pretty well pegged as a shitty excuse for a left-wing propaganda machine. After two days of being dunked on for the original comment, the dunking continued for another two days after he shared the Snopes story, which, apparently, he genuinely believed had vindicated him. Clearly California is not sending their brightest people to Washington, D.C.

Shortly after the 2018 midterm elections, Snopes "fact-checked" an image posted by a right-leaning Facebook group called "Flyover Country." The image in question claimed that Democrats elected "four horrible people" during the midterms, leading Snopes to headline its piece: "Did Democrats Elect Four Horrible People?"[206] The obvious answer is "No." Democrats elected far more than four "horrible people" in November 2018. In fact, the number of Democrats who were elected is precisely the same as the number of horrible people who were elected, and not by coincidence. Snopes again rated this claim as a "mixture" of falsehood and truth.

One of the alleged "horrible people" referenced in the meme was Rep. Alexandria Ocasio-Cortez (D-NY), whom the meme said was "dumber than a salamander." Snopes responded to this claim with an existential diatribe about the intelligence of salamanders. Seriously.

> While the other three claims in this meme were at least rooted in something from conspiracy theory to news reports, the description of Ocasio-Cortez was nothing more than an ad hominem insult. Out of curiosity, however, we attempted to find the average IQ of a salamander but were unable to unearth any credible studies relating to IQ tests for amphibians. IQ tests for humans do exist, but it should be noted that they aren't the best method for measuring intelligence. We weren't able to find any credible reports about Ocasio-Cortez' IQ, but it's reasonable to assume that the youngest woman ever to be elected to the U.S. House of Representatives is more intelligent than your average salamander (and possibly most meme makers to boot).

Thank God Snopes cleared that up. Had they not, Democrats might actually have attempted to substitute Ocasio-Cortez with a salamander to vote in her absence. "A meme on Facebook said they have the same IQ!" Speaker Pelosi would have argued. Then what would we have done? Had a salamander voting in the U.S. Congress? Absurd! By the way, the not-so-subtle dig at the right-wing meme makers is another clue that Snopes is a leftist operation.

But despite the lesson about amphibious IQs, Snopes failed to answer the real question. Is Ocasio-Cortez a "horrible person"? The reader is left to wonder. That is because whether someone is a horrible person versus, say, just a bad person, is a *completely* subjective and opinion-based assessment. It cannot be "fact-checked." The only reason for Snopes to even be involved in this conversation is to cover for Democrats. Which is exactly what they did for the duration of that article.

The other three "horrible people" in question were Sen. Bob Menendez (D-NJ), who has been the subject of speculation regarding sexual misconduct with minors in the Dominican Republic, Rep. Ilhan Omar (D-MN), and Democrat Keith Ellison, the Minnesota Attorney General.

Omar once Tweeted that "Israel has hypnotized the world," and prayed to Allah that he "awaken the people and help them realize the evil doings of Israel."[207]

If anyone on the political right made such a statement, they would be chastised as an anti-Semite relentlessly until their career in politics was finished. In fact, Snopes' counterpart *PolitiFact* called former Republican Senate candidate Corey Stewart an anti-Semite for not adequately denouncing a one-time political ally from years before his Senate campaign who made anti-Semitic remarks years after they associated with each other.[208]

But Snopes let Omar's comments slide, claiming that she was not an anti-Semite (and leaving the reader to draw the conclusion that she is not a "horrible person") because, well, Omar says she's not an anti-Semite.

"Omar has denied her criticisms of Israel are rooted in anti-Semitism," the piece said in her defense.

No need to question any further. The internet truth brigade just told you what to think!

That is not the only time an "I said so" would suffice as proof enough to "fact-check" an internet claim. In the wake of the Las Vegas Massacre, the deadliest shooting in American history that left fifty-eight dead, a Melbourne, Australia Antifa group claimed responsibility for the attack on a Facebook page called "Melbourne Antifa." When *Daily Mail* reported on the post, Snopes was quick to "fact-check" the British news titan, claiming that the Facebook page was not the legitimate "Melbourne Antifa" group, but rather an imposter running a hoax.[209] For this information, Snopes cited an anonymous blogger called "Slackbastard," which, as Snopes reported, was actually a pseudonym for a man named Andy Fleming. Fleming was a supposed "anti-fascist" from the Melbourne area, thus giving him subject matter expertise.

I was unsatisfied with taking Snopes' word for it and curious about this interesting development after such a historic tragedy. Call me crazy, but anonymous bloggers are not exactly known as power brokers of truth. I had a conversation with Fleming about the alleged "fake" Antifa page.[210]

"Well I reckon it was a hoax," he said of the page. "And I should prolly [sic] know."

So I asked him how he knew.

"For a no. [sic] of reasons: I live in Melbourne; I've been participating in anti-fascist activism for years; I know other anti-fascists in Melbourne; I read it; like other fake pages it was a garbagefire [sic]; it appeared along w' a slew of other fake pages."

In other words, Fleming had no clue whether the page was real or fake. He just had a feeling that it was fake. And this is the man whom Snopes used to justify their own claim that the Antifa page was fake. How's that for "fact-checking?"

Part of Snopes' mission is also to suck all of the fun out of the internet, evidenced by their "fact-checking" of articles from known satirical websites. *Babylon Bee* is a niche satire site frequented by many right-wingers. In April 2018, the site published an article ridiculing Planned Parenthood, to which Snopes took offense.[211] The satirical article read:

> While almost nobody is willing to defend Bill Cosby any longer after he was convicted of sexual assault Thursday, the former television star and comedian found an ally in abortion provider Planned Parenthood. President Cecile Richards came forward to claim that since sexual assault is only about 3% of what Bill Cosby performed over his long and illustrious career, the egregious offenses should be overlooked.

The article was an obvious spoof. Planned Parenthood famously claims that while they murder hundreds of thousands of innocent human beings in cold blood, abortion is only 3 percent of what they do as an organization. *Babylon Bee* was pointing out the flawed logic—one horrible act is not remedied by any amount of innocuous acts.

But not all heroes wear capes, and even though the job may be difficult, Snopes could not let *Babylon Bee* get away with making a joke on the web. What if someone took the piece seriously? That could be apocalyptic! How will we ever repay Snopes for their service to society? "Fact-checking" jokes must be quite a thankless task.

"The *Babylon Bee* is an entertainment web site with [sic] long history of publishing satirical articles," Snopes said. "In this case, the web site appears to be spoofing an often-quoted statistic about the nonprofit organization; although many people may equate it with abortion, Planned Parenthood's annual report states that these procedures only make up 3 percent of the medical services that they provide."[212]

All of *Babylon Bee*'s articles are satirical. None of them are factually correct, because that is not the intended goal of the site. The site is not trying to fool anyone into thinking that it provides real news. Satire is meant to be funny, not informative. But it stands to reason that if Snopes is going to "fact-check" one article from *Babylon Bee*, it should "fact-check" them all. Yet Snopes does not do that. They choose which articles from *Babylon Bee* and other such sites to "fact-check" without specified criteria.

How Snopes chooses which satirical articles to "fact-check" remains a mystery, but they sure are keen on killing joy. Sometimes the site will mention that a lot of people have contacted them questioning whether a story is real. In any case, some of the most hilarious (and obviously) satirical articles ever written by *Babylon Bee* have been seriously "fact-checked" by the stiffs at Snopes. Like when they assured the internet that Joel Osteen most certainly did *not* sail his luxury yacht through the city of Houston during Hurricane Harvey passing out copies of his book.[213] Or when they just had to be sure you knew that it is not a federal crime to play Christmas music before Thanksgiving.[214] No wonder I looked like a jackass for calling the cops on my local grocery story when they played "It's Beginning to Look A Lot Like Christmas" in early November. I wish I had found that Snopes article sooner!

Snopes has also fact-checked other obviously satirical claims from decades-old satire site *The Onion*. They proudly debunked a June 2018 *Onion* rumor that ICE agents hurled a pregnant woman over a non-existent border wall so that she would not give birth to an anchor baby.[215] Some other honorable mentions from Snopes' *Onion* "fact-checks" include debunking articles that claimed:

A Detroit judge did not *order a white woman accused of murder to stand trial as a black man.[216]*

Royal Caribbean's M.S. allure did not *sink a Carnival Cruise Lines ship with cannon fire off the coast of The Bahamas in an oceanic territory dispute.[217]*

Hundreds of Cuban refugees did not *physically cling to the underbelly of Air Force One when it flew back to the United States from the island nation in 2016.[218]*

The state of Ohio did not *replace death by lethal injection with a "head ripping off machine" for death row inmates in 2014.[219]*

I would hate to give you the impression that I am only picking on Snopes here, because *PolitiFact* sucks too.

PolitiFact might be worse than Snopes in that it is a project of the Poynter Institute, a decidedly liberal non-profit.[220] Poynter once received a $275,000 donation from notorious left-wing donor and Hungarian-born billionaire George Soros' Tides Foundation, according to Capital Research.[221] The Ford Foundation has also donated $2,415,000 to Poynter since 2000. Among Ford Foundation's other recipients of charitable contributions are Soros' progressive group called the Center for American Progress[222] and David Brock's liberal Media Matters for America.[223] The same groups that are funding America's most outrageously leftist nonprofits in America are also funding Poynter, and thus *PolitiFact*. You are not supposed to know that. You are supposed to believe that *PolitiFact* is totally objective and non-partisan. But it is not.

Here's a fun story. *PolitiFact* "fact-checked" a private citizen's Facebook post shortly before the November 2018 midterm elections.[224] On November 5, the day before the midterm elections, "All In With Chris Hayes" on MSNBC aired a graphic showing a vote tally between Florida gubernatorial candidates

Andrew Gillum and now-Governor Ron DeSantis. The graphic pictured vote totals, percentage of the vote won by each candidate, and even the percentage of the vote that had been counted. It said Gillum won 3,343,634 votes, or 49.4 percent of the vote to DeSantis's 3,297,970 votes, or 48.8 percent of the vote. It even pictured the two candidates side by side and, in the upper right-hand corner, said that 99 percent of the votes had been counted. It looked completely legitimate.

Naturally, with it being the day before the election, some wondered what kind of tomfoolery was going on at MSNBC. Obviously, those could not possibly have been the real results of the election. A concerned citizen shared the graphic in a pro-Trump Facebook group, and *PolitiFact* took it upon themselves to berate the poor lady.

"No, MSNBC didn't call the Florida governor's race for Andrew Gillum before Election Day," the site's headline read.[225] But *nobody even made that claim.* Even in the Facebook post, the woman noted that MSNBC obviously "screwed up." Still, *PolitiFact* made it a point to defend MSNBC.

> *The image actually did air, but the network was quick to say it was an error. (We saw the image that aired on "All In With Chris Hayes" on Nov. 5 at around the 12:15 mark of the episode that was posted to YouTube. Hayes's correction comes around 28:30.). "Quick clarification here," he said. "Earlier this hour we showed a graphic of the Florida gubernatorial race—may have caught your eye because our system had inadvertently populated some test numbers. Obviously, we do not yet have any vote totals here the night before the election. That was*

a misfire. Don't worry, I was pretty confused when I saw it up there."

PolitiFact then stated that the election results were not yet available (The day before the election? You don't say!) and then rated the claim (that no one made) as "False." This was purely public relations work done by *PolitiFact* on behalf of MSNBC. They found some random woman on Facebook who pointed out that MSNBC made a mistake, falsely accused her of saying something she did not say, and then made sure their audience knew that MSNBC absolutely did not say what *PolitiFact* falsely accused the woman of saying.

PolitiFact is also in the business of fact-checking viral internet memes, which, like satirical articles, are not meant to be taken seriously. Nearly 100 percent of internet users know this. Memes are supposed to be comical. Nobody—I cannot emphasize this enough—*nobody* looks to internet memes for serious information. But when someone posted a meme claiming that "If you cross the border illegally in the U.S., you get a driver's license, medical insurance, housing, career training, the right to vote," *PolitiFact* made sure to "fact-check" the viral image.[226]

True, some illegal aliens manage some of these things. Many get drivers licenses. Some bilk the system for health insurance, and some even vote. But the meme was obviously meant to poke fun at liberals who are notoriously soft on illegal immigration. It was shared on a Judge Jeanine Pirro fan page on Facebook. Who on earth looks there for serious information regarding illegal immigration? Nobody.

But the horror of people making jokes on the internet was just too much for *PolitiFact* to handle. The site said:

If someone is caught crossing U.S. borders illegally, they're placed in removal proceedings or returned to their countries. They don't automatically get the benefits outlined in the meme. People who already live in the United States illegally may be able to get some priviliges [sic] such as a driver's license or medical care—if their state allows it, not many do. Those benefits are not guaranteed across the country. Immigrants in the country illegally are barred from federal housing benefits. Children can go to public school regardless of immigration status, though it's unclear if that's what the post suggests by "career training." Only U.S. citizens can vote in federal elections, a few jurisdictions allow noncitizens to participate in local elections.

Internet "fact-checkers" who "correct" non-serious memes are the internet equivalent to those aggravating middle school nerds who took pride in proving the teacher wrong in between eating their own boogers and getting shoved in lockers.

The world of "fact-checkers" is a sorry one, and the term "fact-checker" is a synonym for "Democrat operative." Need proof? Go to Snopes' site and search the term "CNN." See how often the site goes out of its way to prove the Cable News Network wrong, which is not a difficult task. The answer is rarely. Obfuscating the truth in an effort to discredit independent press citizen journalists, and internet meme-makers, all to keep the money-grubbing liars in the corporate press afloat, makes the "fact-checkers" an enemy of the people.

CHAPTER 9

BOMBSHELLS:
THE REAL FAKE NEWS

The mainstream press rarely retracts stories anymore. When they are wrong, which is a frequent occurrence, they issue quiet corrections and move on with their day, hoping nobody notices. Generally, the result is that the original incorrect story gets far more traction than the corrected version. The enemies in the media use this strategy on purpose to fool hapless leftists that consume their garbage. Confusing the public is fine by the corporate media, as long as the end result is damaging to President Trump and Republicans. And since they have already gotten paid in page views and viewership whilst reporting the original fake news, what do they care? False stories are a win-win for a press that only has to appeal to the radical Trump-haters who are willing to believe anything that confirms their ever-so-nuanced worldview that the orange man in the Oval Office is a big fat Russian colluding traitor.

Take a December 2017 CNN story penned by Manu Raju and Jeremy Herb, a supposed "bombshell," as an example. The original story accused President Trump, Donald Trump Jr., and others in the Trump campaign of receiving a "decryption key and website address for hacked Wikileaks documents" by email from a shady internet source on September 4, 2016.[227] But CNN got the date wrong. The date on which Trump Jr. received the information via email was actually ten days later, on September 14, 2016. CNN issued the following correction, while leaving the original story up:

"Correction: This story has been corrected to say the date of the email was September 14, 2016, not September 4, 2016. The story also changed the headline and removed a tweet from Donald Trump Jr., who posted a message about WikiLeaks on September 4, 2016."

No big deal, right? CNN just printed the incorrect date. Actually, the date was a *huge* deal.

Wikileaks, which has been at the center of the bogus Russian "collusion" narrative and accused of working with the Kremlin on behalf of the Trump campaign, publicly released batches of documents, some of which were damaging to the Clinton campaign, throughout the 2016 election season.

One of those document dumps occurred on September 13, 2016, when Wikileaks released a decryption key for the batch of documents on its Twitter account. When CNN released its "bombshell" story claiming that Trump Jr. received the encryption key to secret Wikileaks documents on September 4, it appeared as though the Trump campaign had had foreknowledge of the document release, which suggested that they privately conspired with Wikileaks in an attempt to obtain damaging information on Clinton. In reality, Trump Jr. was made aware of the Wikileaks documents the day after they were released publicly, on September 14. CNN barely made an attempt to provide this context, even in the corrected version of their story.

"The new information indicates that the communication is less significant than CNN initially reported," the story explained.[228] "CNN has now obtained a copy of the email, which lists September 14 as the date sent and contains a decryption key that matches what WikiLeaks had tweeted out the day before."

Less significant? That's putting it mildly. Rightfully, the story should have been retracted. After all, Trump Jr. receiving public information via email is not really newsworthy. But CNN kept the story up because to the naked eye, it still appears that there was some impropriety on behalf of the Trump campaign. Original text from the story that is still live in the updated version even claims that there may have been impropriety, though CNN corrected itself in the preceding paragraphs.

"Sources said Thursday that congressional investigators were trying to ascertain whether the individual who sent the September email is legitimate and whether it shows additional efforts by WikiLeaks to connect with Trump's son and others on the Trump campaign," the article said.

Except there couldn't have been any "additional efforts" on behalf of Wikileaks to connect with the Trump campaign, because there were no efforts in the first place! Why couldn't CNN just take its medicine and admit that in their hasty attempt to slime Trump, they made something up that was completely untrue?

The entire premise behind the Russian "collusion" hoax that has turned the political left into hysterical, apoplectic lunatics will inevitably be outed as a Goebbels-sized lie that would have made the Nazi propagandist proud, and will ruin what precious little credibility that the mainstream press has left. The claim that Trump worked with Vladimir Putin and the Russians to get elected doesn't even makes sense on its face. It does not even withstand the basic test of common sense. It is nothing more than anti-Trump fan fiction befitting for those who have watched so many Hollywood-produced mystery movies that their brains have rotted past the point of functionality.

Riddle me this: Why, pray tell, would Putin need Trump to gain access to the annals of the United States government when he already had a pre-existing relationship with Hillary Clinton? Her State Department sold off 20 percent of America's uranium supply to Russia right around the time when, purely coincidentally, to be sure, Bill Clinton traveled to Russia and gave one of his famous $500,000 speeches.[229] Slick Willy is charismatic, no doubt. Just ask Monica Lewinsky. Maybe he's even so charismatic that one of his famed speeches is worth half a million bucks. But the claim promulgated by the leftist media for two years is that instead of taking the sure bet and teaming up with Hillary, Putin inexplicably decided to work with the dark horse—the man who had the worst odds of getting elected out of *any candidate* when he entered the race, so that he could obtain favors from the United States government that he had already obtained when Clinton was in charge. There has not been one decent explanation for why that would be the case. Maybe instead of prattling on about the sex lives of thirty-something-year-old singles, *The New York Times* could publish a Sunday op-ed explaining this bizarre decision by Putin, for inquiring minds.

But, I digress. There are plenty more non-retractions to cover!

The Wikileaks email story was CNN's follow-up to the false June "bombshell" wherein they predicted that former FBI Director James Comey would testify before Congress and under oath that Trump had "obstructed justice" in the Russian "collusion" probe.[230] The network produced a honking piece of crap that claimed Comey had made it clear to Trump when they spoke, on three occasions, that he was under investigation and that attempts to mislead Comey could be a crime. Trump reportedly asked Comey to "ease up" his investigation into Lt. General Michael Flynn in an Oval Office meeting, and asked Comey to "pledge loyalty" to him.

Had Trump been formally under investigation, the requests he made of Comey might have been out of bounds. CNN went ahead and assumed Comey would corroborate their allegations and tell Congress that Trump knew he was under investigation during the occasions when the pair chatted. Comey did not. In fact, he testified to just the opposite of what CNN reported he would, that Trump was told he was *not* under criminal investigation. Instead of issuing a retraction of the bogus story that intimated the president had acted criminally, CNN simply issued another correction.

"This article was published before Comey released his prepared opening statement," the correction said. "The article and headline have been corrected to reflect that Comey does not directly dispute that Trump was told multiple times he was not under investigation in his prepared testimony released after this story was published."

In other words, CNN was forced to do a complete 180—from claiming that Comey would testify that Trump obstructed justice, to Comey being "unlikely to judge on obstruction." More fantastic work from the *Cable News Network*!

In the "taxpayer-funded lies about Trump" category, a late 2018 botched story by NPR led to another embarrassing correction after the radio outlet claimed Donald Trump Jr. was in serious legal trouble for lying to Senate investigators in 2017.[231] This incorrect story, too, dealt with the Russia probe.

NPR, frothing at the mouth to redeem the rest of the mainstream press and assure Americans that the Trumps are guilty of something related to Russia and the 2016 election—even if they're not sure what—reported that Trump Jr. gave testimony contradicting that of Trump's ex-lawyer Michael Cohen, which Cohen had given in a plea deal exchange with Robert Mueller over financial crimes unrelated to Trump or Russia.

In Trump Jr.'s 2017 Senate testimony, he told investigators about a real estate deal that the family was working on in 2014 that had "faded away," meaning nothing ever came of it. He also told investigators that the family was working on a separate real estate deal to build a Trump Tower Moscow in 2015 and 2016. In Cohen's plea agreement testimony the week of the NPR story, he, too, told investigators about the discussed Trump Tower Moscow deal from 2015 and 2016.

NPR, thinking it had the scoop of the century that would finally end what they surely believe is a reign of Trump tyranny, hustled to publish a story claiming Cohen and Trump Jr.'s testimony conflicted. The radio station accused Trump Jr. of lying to make it seem as though his father's business talks with Russia ended in 2014, when the first deal "faded away." They simply forgot, ignored, or pretended that Trump Jr. had also truthfully testified about the Trump Tower Moscow deal from 2015 and 2016.

NPR, like their comrades at CNN, failed to do the respectable thing and issue a retraction. Instead, they too issued a correction.

"An earlier version of this report mischaracterized an answer Donald Trump Jr. gave to Senate investigators in 2017 about the prospective projects his family was negotiating with people in Moscow," the correction said.

Ordinary people might call NPR's report a lie, considering that the news outlet said something happened when that thing provably did not happen. The enemies of the people, however, called it a "mischaracterization." NPR even kept the original headline, which reads "Cohen's Account of Russia Talks Raises Questions About Trump Jr. 2017 Testimony." That is patently untrue. The only people to whom Cohen's testimony raised questions were the staff at NPR, and that's only because the staff at NPR were apparently too pinheaded to comprehend the transcript of Cohen's testimony.

Then there was the December 1, 2017 report from ABC's Brian Ross about retired Lt. General Michael J. Flynn, the one-time national security advisor to Trump, whom the alphabet network flatly and wrongly claimed was directed by Trump to reach out to the Russians during his presidential bid.[232] The report came on the heels of Flynn making a plea agreement with Mueller for allegedly lying to the FBI during the course of Russia probe. If you're noticing that the subject of many of these fabricated stories involves the alleged Russian "collusion" accusation, that is because no news outlet, no matter how crafty, can manage to write a truthful story about something that never happened. There is no polishing this turd, but ABC still did their damnedest.

"Retired Lt. Gen Michael Flynn has promised 'full cooperation' in the special counsel's Russia investigation and, according to a confidant, is prepared to testify that Donald Trump directed him to make contact with the Russians, initially as a way to work together to fight ISIS in Syria," the report said.

"Confidant" is a fancy D.C. word for "made up source." This story would have been huge for the "collusion" crowd, as it would have at least established some sort of connection between Trump and the Russians during his campaign. But those hoping for Trump's impeachment once again hung their heads in disappointment, as it came to light that Trump made no such request of Flynn until after he was elected. Contacting foreign nations is business as usual for an incoming president, usually called establishing diplomatic relations. Eight hours after the story was published, ABC issued a correction, but not a retraction.

"That source later clarified that during the campaign, Trump assigned Flynn and a small circle of other senior advisers to find ways to repair relations with Russia and other hot spots. It was shortly after the election, that President-elect Trump directed Flynn to contact Russian officials on topics that included working jointly against ISIS," the correction, buried at the bottom of the story, said.

ABC kept most of the original headline, which reads "Flynn prepared to testify that Trump directed him to contact Russians about ISIS, confidant says," but Ross, the author of the article, was suspended for making up a story.

The Washington Post then hastily ran an op-ed by Erik Wemple defending Ross, titled "Why suspend ABC's Brian Ross over Michael Flynn mistake?"[233] Leave it to the jokers at *The Post* to claim that Ross was wronged by a suspension after he tarnished the reputation of a sitting president and, for eight hours, misled the entire country into thinking that the president might be a traitor or Russian asset, crippling whatever trust was left in his employer in the process. Seven months later, Ross was fired from the network.

There are plenty of incorrect mainstream press stories written about subjects besides the Russian "collusion" hoax, too.

In January 2017, shortly after Trump was inaugurated, *The Washington Post* reported that the entirety of the State Department's senior administrative team had resigned in protest of Trump. *The Post* reported that the resignations were "part of an ongoing mass exodus of senior Foreign Service officers who don't want to stick around for the Trump era."[234] CNN would echo a similar story shortly after *The Post* published theirs, while members of the press freaked out. Then-*BuzzFeed* blogger Sheera Frenkel said on Twitter:

"Asked a US diplomat friend how he felt about the resignations at State and the Trump administration so far. His answer, 'We are fucked.'"[235]

But contrary to *The Post*'s alarmist report, only four mid-level State Department officials had resigned. Not only that, they resigned at the request of Trump, who told them that their services would no longer be necessary. It was all, again, part of the normal transition of a new presidential administration.[236]

The Post never updated the story, and Frenkel's Twitter scaremongering was apparently so impressive in the mainstream press community that she was hired away from *BuzzFeed*, a glorified blog, to be a cybersecurity reporter at the former paper of record, *The New York Times*. Apparently, all you have to do to work for the *Times* is claim that the sky is falling anytime the Trump administration does anything, even if the event is completely insignificant. It's not high-quality reporting that they're looking for, but rather dedication to assailing the president at every turn.

Sometimes the mainstream press even manages to write fake news stories that do not involve President Trump, his alleged double-life as a Russian spy, or rumors about the goings-on inside his administration. That is exactly what happened when *The New York Times* blamed Sarah Palin's politics for the shooting of former Democratic U.S. Rep. Gabby Giffords of Arizona.

Giffords was wounded and six people were killed when Jared Loughner opened fire at the congresswoman's public event at a Safeway in Tucson.[237] There was no indication that politics was a motive for the shooting, but you wouldn't know that if you read the *Times*. In a 2017 editorial board op-ed called "America's Lethal Politics,"[238] the *Times* made it a point to equivocate Bernie Sanders supporter James Hodgkinson's attempted mass murder of Congressional Republicans at baseball practice—which nearly killed Rep. Steve Scalise (R-LA)—to the 2011 Giffords shooting.

> *Was this attack evidence of how vicious American politics has become? Probably. In 2011, Jared Lee Loughner opened fire in a supermarket parking lot, grievously wounding Representative Gabby Giffords and killing six people, including a 9-year-old girl. At the time, we and others were sharply critical of the heated political rhetoric on the right. Before the shooting, Sarah Palin's political action committee circulated a map that showed the targeted electoral districts of Ms. Giffords and 19 other Democrats under stylized cross hairs. But in that case no connection to the shooting was ever established.*

The Times actually blamed Palin for the Giffords shooting, because why not use Republicans as a punching bag when it is politically expedient? The problem was that there has never been a political motive for the Giffords shooting. Still, when the public at large noticed the *Times'* blatant error, the paper did not retract their story. Instead they issued a correction which acknowledged that the Giffords comparison to the Hodgkinson shooting was improper.

"An editorial on Thursday about the shooting of Representative Steve Scalise incorrectly stated that a link existed between political rhetoric and the 2011 shooting of Representative Gabby Giffords. In fact, no such link was established," the correction said. "The editorial also incorrectly described a map distributed by a political action committee before that shooting. It depicted electoral districts, not individual Democratic lawmakers, beneath stylized cross hairs."

In plain English, the *Times* said, "We know our story is bullshit, but we're leaving it up anyway. Truth be damned!"

The tactic of publishing false stories only to correct them later is, as usual, calculated by the corporate press. The left-wing media will willingly publish stories that they know could be false in the interest of entertaining their radical audience, only to quietly retract their nonsense later, having reaped the financial benefits of publishing "bombshell" fake news. This tactic is a result of a press that has not been questioned or held accountable for their lies for decades. Only since the meteoric rise of President Trump, who has made it a personal mission to debunk the myths promulgated by the left-wing media, have they had to answer for their recklessness.

Their response has been subpar at best. Even when they are caught blatantly lying to ordinary Americans about issues of the utmost importance, the press often refuses to admit its mistakes. For two years, it has tried to convince the public that the president is an asset of a foreign power. Without a shred of evidence, they have labeled Trump as an enemy of the state. Why shouldn't he do the same to them?

Our media is unconcerned with informing the American people. Rather, it is concerned with propagandizing the public on behalf of the Democratic Party and grifting billions of dollars in the process.

CHAPTER 10

DON'T MENTION IT

Believe it or not, the secret sauce for the mainstream press's creation of enough fake news to sell advertisements is what they *do not* report. In this sense, the term "fake news" can be a misnomer. Most of the time, CNN and the others are not outrightly lying to their viewers and readers. This is not to say that they do not outrightly lie—they certainly do—but in the age of the internet, blatant lies are generally too easy to spot, making them undesirable even for the shameless press.

In some cases, the left-wing media will simply blacklist a story completely and fail to report on it at all. Like when NBC, MSNBC, CNN, ABC, *The New York Times*, *HuffPost* and *The Washington Post* all decided that it was completely non-newsworthy that Farzad Fazeli, a California man, attempted to stab Republican Congressional candidate Rudy Peters at a campaign event. Fazeli, known as a Trump-hater among his peers, would have been successful but for his switchblade, which failed to deploy properly.[239] *The Post,* meanwhile, managed to report that Trump senior policy advisor Stephen Miller used to eat glue in the third grade,[240] and all the others managed to report on the teacher's subsequent suspension for speaking with the media about it, giving the full backstory of Miller's glue-eating habits, of course. But somehow the attempted murder of a Republican candidate for statewide office slipped through the cracks.

Even the blackball strategy is a bit risky, though, as independent news sources will often report stories that the mainstream press would prefer to ignore. The smart independent news sources will also report the fact that the mainstream press failed to pick up the story in question, further discrediting the already-distrusted press.

Instead, the media gets creative.

The main deception tactic that is consistently employed by press giants involves selectively reporting or omitting facts based on how well they fit the desired left-wing narrative. This is the recipe by which mainstream news is made. It is incredibly effective. All the press needs to do in order to keep up the charade is factually report on what is important to the narrative, leave out what is factually correct but not important to the narrative, and continue to sell the biggest lie of all—that they are "unbiased" news sources.

In November 2018, mainstream press jumped all over a story about Ivanka Trump using a personal email account to discuss official government business. Immediately, the "whataboutisms," the line of argumentation that justifies or condemns the actions of one person based on the actions of another, began. And the press condemned the hell out of Ivanka. "What about when President Trump bashed Hillary Clinton for her email scandal?" the press whined. CNN reported the following:

[Ivanka] Trump's usage of a private email account will bring comparisons to former Secretary of State Hillary Clinton, whose usage of a private email server instead of a government email account during her time in office was a central part of President Donald Trump's campaign against her in 2016. Trump's supporters often chanted -- and still do, on occasion -- "Lock her up!" at the mention of Clinton, and President Donald Trump has frequently accused Clinton of receiving special treatment because she was not charged for skirting the Presidential Records Act with her email practices.[241]

Can you spot the conspicuously missing facts that an honest media would have reported in this situation? Ivanka and Clinton's stories are exactly the same—but for the fact that Clinton used an unsecured internet server, and sent and received classified information via her private email and unsecured server.[242] Clinton later deleted 33,000 of those emails, which had been subpoenaed by investigators,[243] then bleached her hard drives and smashed them with hammers to hide the evidence.[244]

While Ivanka bent the rules, Clinton broke the rules in half and stomped all over them. Clinton's case was a matter of national security, not a matter of what email address she used. But an honest comparison of the situations would have ruined that narrative put forth by the press: that Ivanka and Clinton did the *same* thing. CNN failed to report on the important differences in the two scenarios, instead choosing the route that would allow them to attack President Trump and would allow airheads to create a false equivalency between

Clinton and Ivanka's actions. And falsely equivocate the airheads did.

"Dear Donald, Where are the 'Lock her up' chants? What are you waiting for? 'Lock her up! Lock her up!'" said the political left's most successful internet grifter Brian Krassenstein, on his Twitter account.[245]

"'Most people realize that government officials do use their private e-mail occasionally,'" said CNN's Jeffrey Toobin according to left-wing *Mediaite*.[246] "'Hillary Clinton did it, too. It is not fundamentally a big deal. The news media made it a big deal. Donald Trump made it a big deal... It's technically not within the rules, but everybody in government does it. This is the problem. This is why Hillary Clinton got a very raw deal.'"

There it is again, the whole ignoring-relevant-facts-to-push-the-narrative thing. In this case, *Mediaite* quoted CNN. The shape-shifted narrative has a compounding effect. It is repeated by the entirety of the left-wing mainstream press until it becomes reality. From this point forward, the unthinking masses will be talking about how Ivanka "committed the same crime as Hillary," thanks to their programming by CNN and others. The media is purposefully conflating the two scenarios out of a desperation for clicks and page views, both of which keep their businesses solvent. Who cares whether the truth is lost in the shuffle? Who cares that this will be a new point of contention between Americans in an already-rocky political climate? The fat cats in the mainstream media game need their bonuses this quarter! On top of that, they get to knock Trump and his supporters down a few pegs. Tell us more about how you're our friends, CNN!

Sadly, you can find examples of this tactic in nearly every news story that exists on the web today.

The most blatant example of narrative creation by the mainstream press is illustrated by America's seemingly everlasting debate on immigration. The narrative promulgated by the press is that Republicans, especially Trump, hate all immigrants. And since the press has decided that every immigrant to the United States is nonwhite, the subtext of the narrative is that Republicans are bigoted racists, too. Trump has never once tied race to immigration—nor has he ever denounced immigration as a whole. In fact, he has made it abundantly clear that America welcomes immigrants that come here *legally*. That small, but very reasonable nuance, appears lost on the cosmopolitan literati.

The New York Times compiled a handy guide called "Trump's Immigration Policies Explained" in February 2017.[247] The paper explained that Obama categorized certain illegal aliens, like felons or prior deportees, as high priority. That policy allowed for the deportation of those illegals, but the run-of-the-mill illegal was protected from deportation if they were not a member of one of these high priority groups. Bear in mind that all illegals, regardless of whether they have racked up other crimes while here illegally, are still breaking the law. As you might imagine, this policy of prioritizing certain lawbreakers over others was frustrating for Immigrations and Customs Enforcement (ICE) agents. In tens of thousands of instances, it defeated the purpose of their job completely. They would scoop up illegal aliens only to be forced to let them go because, aside from breaking the law by crossing the border illegally, those illegals had not broken the law.

"Under the new directives, the government 'no longer will exempt classes or categories of removable aliens from potential enforcement,'" the *Times* explained. "Immigration agents can now focus on picking up and removing anyone charged with or convicted of any criminal offense, even minor ones, as well as anyone already ordered deported, regardless of whether they have a criminal record."

Plainly speaking, the "new" rules set forth by the Trump administration said that illegal border hoppers could be deported for any criminal offense, including hopping the border illegally. What a novel idea!

The "new" rules weren't new at all. They're actually the old rules. The ones that had been in place forever before the lawless Obama administration.

But the *New York Times* left that part out. An honest press would have simply noted that Trump plans to enforce immigration laws as written. *The Times* wanted its audience to think that Trump and his Republicans are targeting illegals with some twisted new scheme, thought up by a group of old white men in some ivory tower while they sat around drinking scotch and chortling. Not only that, the *Times* left the word "illegal" out of their headline. The piece explained Trump's plans for illegal immigrants, not simply "immigrants," as the headline suggested. Make no mistake, the subtle conflation of illegal aliens with legal immigrants is a coordinated and intentional tactic used by the press to magnify Trump hatred. Nobody is rounding up legal immigrants who have committed crimes, despite what the *Times* would have you think.

A little bit of tugging at the heartstrings, and the *Times'* goal of demonizing Trump to promote the "Republicans hate immigrants" narrative is achieved.

"One unauthorized immigrant in California, Kristina, who did not want her last name used because of fear of deportation, said she was alarmed to learn on Tuesday that she would now be considered a prime target," the paper said.

Apparently, Kristina had been breaking America's laws for twenty-five years. Her whole life was here. Her kids were here. If deported, her life might become difficult. How dare that evil Trump and his Republican henchmen be so bold as to enforce border laws, like every other sane nation on planet earth! We can't have that in progressive America!

In the run up to the 2018 midterm elections, a Republican PAC ran television ads featuring illegal alien and cop killer Luis Bracamontes. Bracamontes, an illegal from Mexico, made headlines not when he opened fire on several sheriff's deputies in Northern California in 2014, killing two and injuring two more.[248] Illegals killing police officers is not a narrative that the press is interested in furthering. After all, Democrats love illegal immigration. Rather, Bracamontes, who had also been previously convicted and deported on drug and weapons-related offenses in 1997 and 2001, made headlines only when he was the subject of the attack ad.[249] The ad was meant to highlight the fact that illegals can, and often do cause trouble in the United States—trouble that could be altogether avoided if we enforced our border laws. Bracamontes can be seen in the ad smiling and laughing in court after being convicted in the killing of the police officers. He told the court that he wished he had killed more police officers, and that he would do just that if ever released from prison. The ad was effective, so the press went into attack mode.

When Trump shared the ad in a Tweet, the media lost its collective mind. It was quickly dubbed "racist" and "anti-immigrant" by the press. Even Fox was goaded into rebuking the ad.

"NBC and Fox News said in separate statements on Monday that their networks will no longer air the Trump campaign's racist anti-immigrant advertisement," said a CNN article.[250]

"NBC, Fox News and Facebook pulled a widely-condemned anti-immigrant ad by President Donald Trump's campaign as a bitter election fight for control of the US Congress headed on Monday for an unpredictable finish," Qatari owned *Al-Jazeera* reported.[251]

"NBC, Fox News, Facebook pull controversial Trump anti-immigration ad," read an Axios headline.[252]

ABC published an op-ed titled "How Trump's controversial anti-immigrant video skirts rules for political ads."[253] Apparently, ABC is making the "rules" for political advertising now.

Not only was the ad unrelated to the "Trump campaign" (Trump was not even campaigning in 2018, but these are minor details), there was nothing remotely "racist" or "anti-immigrant" about it. The ad did not even mention Bracamontes's race. Neither did Trump. Only the media did that. Worse still, the ad's stated purpose was to warn of the dangers of unvetted illegal aliens crossing America's borders. That message was explicit. The ad was not made to deride immigrants who come to America legally, follow the proper protocols, wait in line, and pay thousands of dollars. Nor was it made to attack anyone on the basis of race. But again, the nuance does not fit the narrative, so the press left the nuance out.

Ordinary Americans understand the difference between legal and illegal immigration. After all, it is not a complicated dichotomy to grasp. The only people who seem to have a difficult time grasping the difference are those who work in the mainstream press.

Not only do regular people understand the difference, they feel very strongly about the topic. According to a 2013 Center for Immigration Studies poll, 52 percent of Americans believe that illegal immigrants should be deported back to their home countries, versus only 33 percent who believe that they should be allowed to stay. Further, there is a huge enthusiasm gap between the people who hold these beliefs. Of the majority of people who believe illegals should be deported, 73 percent felt "very strongly" about their opinion. Of the minority who believed that illegals should stay, only 35 percent felt "very strongly" about their opinion.[254] The mainstream press is part of this tiny minority—the 35 percent of the 33 percent who feel "very strongly" that illegal aliens should be able to break America's laws with impunity.

The way CNN, NBC, and the other cable news clowns swoon over illegals, you would think that Americans were dying to have their neighborhoods invaded by hordes of strangers who don't speak their language or understand their customs. The vast majority are not. Unfortunately, the small minority has the megaphone. The most extreme faction of insane leftists is screaming the loudest, calling the majority "racist" and "xeno-phobic." Still wondering why Trump calls the media the enemy of the people?

The demented spin from the mainstream press—all in the name of the desired narrative—prompted Trump to fire back.

"We have forcefully condemned hatred, bigotry, racism and prejudice in all of its ugly forms, but the media doesn't want you to hear your story. It's not my story. It's your story. And that's why 33 percent of the people in this country believe the fake news is, in fact—and I hate to say this—in fact, the enemy of the people," he said.[255]

Speaking of foreign invaders, chronically omitted by the mainstream press in the name of furthering "progressivism" in America are the human rights atrocities of radical Islam, a religion that has increasingly and worryingly permeated American culture. There is a distinct and emerging trend of left-wing media propping up unsavory figures like Linda Sarsour, a fundamental Islamist, as some sort of champion for women's rights and progressive values. Congresswomen Rashida Tlaib (D-MI) and Ilhan Omar (D-MN) have likewise been celebrated by the mainstream press for bringing "diversity" and "progressivism" to the legislature.

The narrative, of course, is that diversity is America's strength, that diversity is inextricably tied to progressivism, and that diversity certainly does not exist within the Republican party, which consists only of old white men. Since diversity and progressivism are meant to be celebrated, anyone who questions this narrative is then slandered by the same press that created the narrative, and called a bigot or a racist.

But if ever there was a case of cognitive dissonance in media, this is it. There is *nothing* even remotely "progressive" about radical Islam. Sharia Law, practiced in the strictest of Islamic nations, is a barbaric practice that is responsible for ongoing human rights abuses. The media conveniently forgets about these abuses whenever a woman in a hijab parrots a "progressive" talking point.

TIME Magazine even named Sarsour as one of 2017's one hundred "most influential people."[256] Sarsour founded the Women's March that year in Washington, D.C., in protest of Trump's entire existence. In the gushing *TIME* piece, written by Sen. Kirsten Gillibrand (D-NY), Sarsour was described with cult-like fetishism.

"The images of Jan. 21, 2017, show a diverse, dynamic America—striving for equality for all. The moment and movement mattered so profoundly because it was intersectional and deeply personal," the piece said. "This is the rebirth of the women's movement. These women are the suffragists of our time. And our movement isn't going away—it's just the beginning."

The last thing that radical Islamists believe in is "equality for all." For the sake of the women in this country, I sure hope radical Islamist Linda Sarsour is not going to be leading their next "suffrage." If that's the case, they stand a chance of living in a place where adulterers are stoned to death, like the women who live under Islamic law in countries like Saudi Arabia.[257] Only in 2018 did that Islamic nation lift its ban on females driving cars,[258] but female drivers still must be accompanied by a husband or male family member. It's also the same nation and

Islamic law that was responsible for forty-eight beheadings in the first four months of 2018—half of them for nonviolent drug offenses.[259] The new "progressive" America that the media is bucking for should be swell!

One of Sarsour's self-proclaimed "mentors" is Brooklyn Imam Siraj Wahhaj, who is an unindicted co-conspirator in the 1993 World Trade Center bombings. The man is quite literally a radical Islamic terrorist. His son, Siraj Ibn Wahhaj, was arrested in summer 2018 along with four other Islamic fundamentalists for running a jihadi training camp in New Mexico, where children were allegedly being taught to carry out mass shootings at hospitals and schools.[260] A year before that revelation, Sarsour addressed the 54th annual Islamic Society of North America Convention in Chicago. She said:

> And to my favorite person in this room, that's mutual, is Imam Siraj Wahhaj, who has been a mentor, motivator, and encourager of mine. Someone who has taught me to speak truth to power, and not worry about the consequences. Someone who has taught me that we are on this Earth to please Allah and only Allah, and that we are not here to please any man or woman on this earth. So I am grateful to you Imam Siraj, and you might think this is weird, but every once in a while, when I get into that deep dark place, Imam Siraj comes and talks to me. And he helps me to emerge out of those places, so I'm grateful to you Imam Siraj, and may Allah bless you and protect you for a long time for our community, because we need you now more than ever.

High praise for a man who hates this country with every fiber of his being and intended to kill as many of us as possible in 1993.

Not only is Sarsour a sympathizer for a horribly backwards ideology, she is rabidly anti-Semitic, a fact which the press seems to finally be noticing after years of warnings from ordinary Americans. Her Women's March organization hobnobs with Louis Farrakhan's Jew-hating Nation of Islam.[261] Farrakhan compared Jews to termites in 2018.[262] Naturally, the press gave him a pass for his comments, because he is a Democrat. How "progressive."

Tlaib, the daughter of Palestinian immigrants, draped herself in a Palestinian flag and danced around with her Islamic compadres when she was officially elected to the United States Congress in November.[263] It seems like the American flag would have been more appropriate.

Unsurprisingly, the press is also silent on the human rights abuses in Palestine. A two-year investigation by Human Rights Watch concluded that "scores" of Palestinian dissenters are arrested, beaten, and tortured by the Palestinian Authority (PA) for broadly defined crimes like insulting a "higher authority."

"The arrests for nonviolent speech acts constitute serious violations of international human rights law, in contravention of legal obligations imposed through Palestine's accession to major international human rights treaties over the last five years. The torture as practiced by both the PA and Hamas may amount to a crime against humanity, given its systematic practice over many years," according to the Human Rights Watch report.[264]

That is what Tlaib was celebrating when she was elected to represent Americans as one of a few hundred lawmakers in the U.S. House of Representatives. Not a peep from our highly-regarded media on the potential danger Tlaib might pose to Jewish-Americans as a lawmaker, considering her sympathies to human rights violators in Palestine. That does not fit the desired narrative.

Omar is a Somali-born immigrant living in Minnesota, the only place where the hijab serves a practical purpose—keeping one warm in sub-zero temperatures. In other places, it is viewed as a symbol of female oppression, which is why daring Iranian women are currently tearing them off in protest of their country's Islamic totalitarianism.[265] She spoke at a pro-Hamas fundraiser disguised as a humanitarian gala for Palestinians during her congressional campaign. The "Dear Gaza Azume Dinner" was held to "provide urgent medical care for the people of the Gaza Strip while celebrating Palestinian culture." Hamas is a designated terrorist organization and controls the Gaza Strip. Any funding or humanitarian aid for the people in Gaza is routed through Hamas.[266]

While campaigning, she claimed that she did not support the Boycott, Divestment and Sanctions (BDS) movement against the state of Israel, calling the movement "counteractive." Immediately after her election she changed her tune and announced her support for the movement.[267]

A fair and honest media would be skeptical of the fact that women calling themselves "progressive" willfully practice the least progressive religion in the world, and embrace an ideology whose stated goal is to destroy America, kill all nonbelievers in the name of Allah, and convert any survivors to Islam. But the media is neither fair nor honest, and they earn a solid living pandering to retarded, self-loathing white liberals who harbor hatred for Christianity. As usual, they simply omit relevant, factual information about radical Islam that could lead to critical thought or discourse about what is best for America, instead opting for such substance as "Look at these brown women! Diversity is a strength! You go girls!"

Much of the press narrative surrounding race is predicated on this bogus idea that diversity is inherently a strength of the United States. But if you ask a Democrat to explain how diversity is a strength, you'll likely get a jumbled word salad in response. That is why no one in media discusses this topic. We are all supposed to simply accept the phrase as a fact and move on, or be labeled a "racist."

But to suggest skin color is at all related to the strength of the United States is condescending. As an Arab-American, I can assure you that the brown-ish tint of my skin is completely irrelevant in measuring the strength of this fine nation. The only characteristic that is relevant to measuring America's strength is each person's individual contribution to society. The neo-Marxist idea that groups of non-white people should be treated as a monolith, and that by just being born non-white they make America stronger, is insulting. It discredits extraordinary individuals of all races who accomplish extraordinary things. The phrase "diversity is a strength" is pushed by the shallow leftist press only to grift for Democrat votes among minorities.

The careful omission of relevant facts that would hurt the leftist media narrative that Republicans are evil and Democrats forward-thinking and compassionate is everywhere. There is not a single news topic that is unaffected by some sort of hoodwinking or spin.

Gun violence exists because Americans own a lot of guns, the media says—consistently failing to mention that 97.8 percent of mass shootings happen in gun-free zones,[268] or that the American cities with the most restrictive gun laws have the most gun homicides. We must ban "military grade assault rifles" like AR-15s, though AR-15s are not military grade or assault rifles, assault rifles were banned in 1994 (and twice before that),[269] and only 3.4 percent of gun homicides are committed with rifles.[270] Abortion equals a woman's right to healthcare, though abortion is not healthcare inasmuch as 100 percent of the patients die, and neither abortion nor healthcare are Constitutional rights.

These are but a few examples of constantly recurring debates that pop up in national media. If it can omit facts on this huge scale, imagine what the press is hiding from you in their exclusive stories, or the stories that are anonymously sourced by shadowy unnamed figures.

Lying by omission is indeed lying. But the press will not stop omitting relevant facts anytime soon. If they do, the left wing's entire narrative will collapse. It is a house of cards that has no foundation in reality. The press carefully crafts stories that are intentionally molded to shape reality through a warped left-leaning lens.

CHAPTER 11

NO-BRAINERS

Before I became a reporter, I thought that members of the D.C. press and punditry class possessed some sort of wizardly quality that consumers of news did not possess. Shortly after I became a reporter, I realized what that quality was: brainlessness. Left-wing D.C. newsies are objectively the dumbest people on earth. Tangentially related is the fact that they're terrible human beings. They're liars, scoundrels, wretches, miscreants, and none of their mothers loved them. If you thought bacteria were the lowest form of life, you ought to hang around Capitol Hill and chat with some members of the mainstream press. They make bacteria look polished and intelligent.

Of course, their target audience is the radical Democrat, and they have to play at the level of this audience, otherwise no one would watch. If nobody watches, nobody gets paid. But once you get trapped in that yellow-padded room of leftist feebleness, your chances of recovery are slim. Remember this objective fact the next time your mind is numbed by the vapidness of a mainstream news segment: our press is complicit in the dumbing down of America.

Leftist *ThinkProgress* recently ran a piece titled "Romaine lettuce is too dangerous to be in stores, but guns are still available 24/7."[271]

"On Thanksgiving Day 2018, Americans couldn't buy romaine lettuce because of a CDC recall linked to an E. Coli outbreak," said the site's Ryan Koronowski. "But even though gun violence is so mundane that a shooting at a mall in Alabama Thursday evening barely made national news, guns were still freely available at stores like Walmart across the country."

See what I mean about the bacteria? The E. Coli couldn't have produced a worse non-sequitur. Apparently thinking is not a prerequisite for working at *ThinkProgress*, despite the name of the publication. For the logically impaired, there are several reasons why romaine was banned, but firearms get to stay. And in case anyone from *ThinkProgress* stumbles upon this book (and knows how to read), the reason is *not* because we don't eat firearms.

Here in America, we have this founding document called the Constitution. It has an addendum called the Bill of Rights. The Bill of Rights originally consisted of ten amendments to the Constitution. The amendments are rights, granted to Americans by God, and protected by the government. The second of those amendments is the right to keep and bear arms. It allows Americans to buy weapons and stockpile ammunition (which you all should be doing gratuitously) on the off chance that government gets out of line and a bunch of us want to get together and do something about it. The placement of the

Second Amendment is key. It's right there at the top of the list, just after the First Amendment, and just before the Third. Those who wrote the Constitution and later the Bill of Rights understood the importance of allowing citizens to defend themselves from a potentially tyrannical government. Now, perhaps the fine fellas who wrote the Bill of Rights were not as forward-thinking as the soy macchiato-drinking staff at *ThinkProgress*, but they did not see fit to squeeze in an amendment protecting garden vegetables in the case of a bacteria outbreak. Thus, the feds can restrict the purchase of salad ingredients as they please. Restricting the purchase of firearms, however, is a bit more complicated. Banning firearms outright will never happen, unless Eric Swalwell decides to nuke us.

And that is where lettuce and firearms differ, at least in the context of this conversation. For most Americans, this is a no-brainer in the proverbial sense. For the left-wing press, it is apparently a no-brainer inasmuch as our distinguished purveyors of information might be missing the organ between their ears.

Sometimes mainstream press figures don't even bother to type out their boneheaded ideas. That would require at least a little bit of brainpower. In 2012, CNN's Fareed Zakaria decided to take the copy/paste route in a plagiarized article about gun control that he ripped from historian Jill Lepore, who originally published her piece in the *The New Yorker*.[272]

"Laws banning the carrying of concealed weapons were passed in Kentucky and Louisiana in 1813, and other states soon followed…. Similar laws were passed in Texas, Florida, and Oklahoma. As the governor of Texas explained in 1893, the 'mission of the concealed deadly weapon is murder,'" Lepore originally wrote.[273]

Zakaria copied the passage for a *Time Magazine* article called "The Case for Gun Control." Zakaria was a contributor at *Time* and *The Washington Post*, and a full-time employee at CNN, when the plagiarism occurred. He was suspended from both outlets while they investigated the matter. He apologized, calling the event a "serious lapse and one that is entirely my fault." (Who else's fault could it have been?)

Time briefly suspended Zakaria, but not before contradicting his own apology and calling his plagiarism "unintentional."

"We have completed a thorough review of each of Fareed Zakaria's columns for TIME, and we are entirely satisfied that the language in question in his recent column was an unintentional error and an isolated incident for which he has apologized," a *Time* spokesperson reportedly said.[274]

How one unintentionally copies the work of another is beyond comprehension. Maybe those wizardly D.C. journalist powers do exist after all.

A month later, Zakaria was reinstated by the ever-principled CNN, too, where he hosts his own show called "Fareed Zakaria GPS." He also still writes a weekly column for *The Washington Post*. There is a joke to be had in here somewhere about moral compasses and GPS.

Two years later, Zakaria was again accused of plagiarism by anonymous bloggers, who noted that twelve of his pieces which appeared in *Time* and CNN looked similar to work written elsewhere.[275] The claims prompted an investigation from CNN. Zakaria had left *Time* before the second round of accusations.

He denied the allegations, saying that the posts in question were not copied, but rather they used statistics that were readily available and published in several places.

Two months after those allegations, *The Week* did a follow-up piece and noted that seven of Zakaria's *Newsweek* columns, one of his *Slate* columns, and four of his *Washington Post* columns had been "affixed with editor's notes essentially admitting to acts of plagiarism" after the same anonymous bloggers called him out for plagiarism in those outlets, too. Ultimately, CNN would let all of the accusations fade into oblivion, relying on the short attention spans of their readership.[276]

How about this no-brainer: Megan McArdle, a Trump-hating neoliberal columnist currently of *The Washington Post,* wrote an opinion piece in *The Daily Beast* in 2012, shortly after the Sandy Hook massacre, wherein she gave her bizarre take on what students should do in the event that their school is overrun by a gun-toting lunatic.

"I'd also like us to encourage people to gang rush shooters, rather than following their instincts to hide; if we drilled it into young people that the correct thing to do is for everyone to instantly run at the guy with the gun, these sorts of mass shootings would be less deadly, because even a guy with a very powerful weapon can be brought down by 8-12 unarmed bodies piling on him at once," she said in the column.[277]

Alternative idea: Don't do this. Bullets hurt. Try avoiding them instead.

This is the depth of the typical Washington, D.C. political writer. Out of all of the possibilities for preventing or lessening the impact of school shootings, McArdle could only come up with "run towards the shooter"? What about, say, armed security guards in schools? How about protecting our children with the same vigor with which we protect banks and federal government buildings, where good guys with guns are ready to take out bad guys with guns at a moment's notice? Nope. Not in the cards for McArdle. The best solution she could come up with was "take one for the team." Truly astounding.

Sometimes when the networks in D.C. run out of airheads to book for their shows, or when they want to attract page views using people who are more attractive than the average political reporter (a mangy bunch), they outsource to Hollywood where they find washed-up celebrities to rehash today's manufactured outrage. It's a sensible crossover, considering that cable news is basically fiction and actors share the same level of political expertise as reporters and political pundits. Realistically, it's all the same.

One of the media's favorite celebrity commentators is Alyssa Milano. Armed with a Twitter account and zero mastery of any political subject, the *Charmed* actress is the perfect crossover pundit. She also hates guns and Trump, so she was whisked through the door at CNN without so much as an interview, and dubbed America's next top commentator.

Back in July 2018, there was some outrage about 3D printable weaponry being made available to the public. The technology is still not polished, and 3D printers of the caliber available to produce a weapon are hugely expensive. But the media loves to fear monger for clicks, so when the State Department settled in court with a 3D weapon blueprinter, allowing him to proceed with the sale of his blueprints, CNN trotted out an opinion piece from Milano.

"Imagine this: the convicted domestic abuser next door tries to buy a gun," she wrote. "He's turned down because he fails his background check. When he gets home, he opens up his browser, and in half an hour he's printing out his own undetectable, fully functional plastic gun, with no background check and no record of his purchase."[278]

Let's slow down for a second. Assuming that one already possesses the costly printer and plastic cutouts required for the use of such a printer, there is far more to the equation than Milano lets on in her rant. For example, there is no such thing as a "fully functional plastic gun." Even 3D printed weapons require metal parts. So, the "domestic abuser next door" would have to purchase those parts, and then use his presumed engineering degree to put them all together. This is not IKEA furniture we're talking about here. There is no all-inclusive package for 3D printed firearms. Milano had no idea, though, because she is absolutely clueless on the subject. She obviously didn't even bother with so much as a Google search before she wrote this piece, and neither did her editors at CNN before they published it. Milano doesn't even know anything about normal firearms. She is part of the class of gun-control morons that believes the "AR" in AR-15 stands for "assault rifle."

Later in the piece, Milano attempted to downplay the costliness of printing such a weapon by saying that it can be done with as little as $2000, proving that she, too, is completely out of touch with ordinary Americans. She fits right in with the D.C. political class!

Nearly 60 percent of Americans have less than $1000 to their name.[279] It doesn't seem like most of us have the requisite budget for the 3D printing of weaponry in the event of a failed background check. By the way, what kind of previous felon would make it a point to come by a firearm honestly? Wouldn't he just steal one? Or buy a stolen one illegally on Craigslist for like fifty bucks? What fantasy world is Milano living in here?

The best part of the piece, though, was when she ventured into hyperbolic territory.

"It is not hyperbole to say that this could mean the end of our ability to have meaningful gun violence prevention in America," she said.

Yes it is. Whenever someone begins a sentence with "It is not hyperbole..." rest assured that whatever follows will be hyperbole. The day after Milano's piece was published, a federal judge ordered the halt of the distribution of 3D firearm blueprints, and just like that "gun violence prevention" was back![280] No hyperbole here!

Milano has plenty of other uninformed opinions on topics other than the Second Amendment that the press will gladly peddle. She penned an opinion piece during the Brett Kavanaugh outrage cycle decrying Trump's judicial appointments, in which she suddenly became an expert on the Judiciary Branch.

"It doesn't end with Kavanaugh on the Supreme Court, though. Donald Trump and Mitch McConnell are waging war against women in the lower courts, ramming through extremist judge after extremist judge in a cowardly assault against a women's [sic] reproductive freedom," she said.[281]

In this context, Milano used "extremist" interchangeably with "conservative," and "reproductive freedom" interchangeably with "infanticide." The piece, which was also totally non-hyperbolic, was published by *Refinery29*, and reported on by larger media outlets like CNN and *USA Today*. In her six hundred or so words about the Judiciary, never did she mention the constitutional right to a trial by jury that was not afforded to Kavanaugh while Democrats shamelessly and falsely accused a decent man of unprovable crimes for political gain. He was judged solely in the court of public opinion, which Milano encouraged.

In less formal political commentary, Milano often uses her Twitter account to berate Trump with profanity-laced soliloquies. Milano got herself in a tizzy when tear gas was deployed to disperse a crowd of five hundred Central American migrants who attempted to cross the U.S. Southern border by rushing the fence last November.

"You tear-gassed women and children, asswipe! And on Thanksgiving weekend, you piece of shit, asshole, motherfucking, evil-creature-person!!" she Tweeted eloquently to her nearly 3.5 million followers.[282]

The internet took her to task, though, noting that in 2013, the same law enforcement entity used the same tactic against about a hundred illegals who attempted to use the "strength in numbers" strategy to cross the border illegally. Like the migrants in 2018, this group, too, hurled bottles and rocks at border patrol agents. Milano and the mainstream press alike mentioned nothing of the 2013 incident, because a Democrat was president. They were dead silent. But under President

Trump, the press turned border security into a human rights issue because they hate Republicans, and they are your enemy.

By the way, there is not a single Central American country that celebrates Thanksgiving, in case you were wondering why that was relevant to the Tweet.[283] Either Milano is uncultured enough to think that every country on earth celebrates what is a primarily American holiday, or she added it into her Tweet purely to ratchet up emotional response from her followers.

Director Rob Reiner is another one of these Hollywood cockroaches who has a great deal of clout with the D.C. media. *The Daily Beast* interviewed Reiner for a wildly conspiratorial piece where he managed to attack Trump for calling the press the "enemy," which he said was an attack on the free press, while simultaneously attacking *Breitbart*, Alex Jones, and others as purveyors of false information who should not be trusted, all while declaring with certainty that Trump is a Russian asset. Reiner said:

> "Because you've got a big chunk of mainstream media—Fox, Sinclair, Breitbart, *Alex Jones and all those groups*—who are basically spinning a completely different narrative than the 60 percent mainstream press. And the people getting their information from that alternative universe, you can't get to them. As a result, we've got this big, big problem in this country of, how do you get through? You've got Vladimir Putin coming along and exploiting that division and hardening that division, because he has an asset there in the president."[284]

This is myopic Hollywood commentary at its finest. According to Reiner, when Trump attacks the leftist corporate press, Trump is attacking the "free press," but when Reiner attacks the alternative media, Reiner is not attacking the "free press." That's pretty convenient "logic." Reiner made his deeply held beliefs quite evident in this interview. If he had his way, media consumption would be restricted only to the cable news networks and other leftist mainstream press that he deems trustworthy. Somehow, in his mind, restrictions on consumable media comport with freedom. On top of that, Reiner is absolutely certain that Trump is in cahoots with the Russian government because those same news outlets told him so, despite having zero proof to support that claim.

That was not the first time that Reiner made puzzling comments about the media in relation to Trump. He appeared on ABC's "The View" where he said that Trump was the first president to be "supported by mainstream media."[285]

"This is the first time also in American history where we have had a president—every president uses propaganda to sell a policy—Republicans and Democrats," he said. "But this is the first time we have had a president that is supported by mainstream media. I mean, Fox is mainstream media."

Was Reiner comatose during the Obama administration? That is some next-level no-brainer bullshit! CNN, NBC, MSNBC, ABC, CBS, and every website from *HuffPost* to *Slate* babied Obama for eight years. It was a cringeworthy display. They openly declared—and still do to this day—that they miss Obama. They could not get enough of charismatic Barry and his hip family. They covered for him at every turn, like when they failed to report on the "human rights violation" of using teargas to fend off foreign invaders. Kudos to "The View" for that segment, though. They might have booked the only guest on planet earth who is foolish enough to believe that the media was not friendly to Obama and company. At the very least, they found the only guest on planet earth shameless enough to spout such a huge lie without becoming embarrassed.

During the same interview, Reiner curiously complained about *Breitbart* and *InfoWars* again, but called them "mainstream press," which is anything but accurate and also the opposite of what he said in his interview with *The Daily Beast*. He seems to lack an understanding of America's media landscape, making him the perfect guest for the mainstream press.

Variety also provided Reiner with an outlet to lash out against Trump.

"Donald Trump is the single most unqualified human being to ever assume the presidency of the United States. He is mentally unfit. Not only does he not understand how government works, he has no interest in trying to find out how it works," Reiner told the magazine.[286]

That argument of "mental fitness" is one of the more egregiously brainless assertions made by liberal commentators and Hollywood celebrities to bash the president, mainly because they have no standing to assess such fitness. They are not doctors, even if they play them on television. How would they know what Trump's level of mental fitness is at all, never mind if it meets the threshold for him to lead this nation? Then again, there is no such threshold. The only "fitness" test the president must pass is decided by the citizens of this country on Election

Day, and it's measured in Electoral College votes. When a candidate wins 270 such votes, he has been deemed fit for office, mentally and otherwise, regardless of what Rob Reiner thinks.

Singer Rihanna recently decided to participate in national political discourse. It turns out that she's no political scholar either. On Instagram (where all Americans turn for nuanced political debate) she captioned a photo of the tear-gassing during the aforementioned migrant border invasion with the word "terrorism," making the mainstream press giddy.[287] It was a brilliant one-word analysis, except for the fact that America defending her borders from foreign invaders does not remotely fit the definition of terrorism. Last time I checked, it was completely lawful for any nation to defend its borders from foreign invasion, and if it isn't, then why bother having borders in the first place?

For Rihanna's reference, a few recent examples of actual terrorism include a radical Islamist ISIS member stabbing five people, one fatally in Paris in the name of Allah,[288] a radical Islamic ISIS-linked gunman taking several French citizens hostage and killing three of them, also in the name of Allah,[289] and a radical Islamic ISIS member opening fire on a police bus in Paris, killing one and wounding three, once again in the name of Allah.[290]

As we all know, Hollywood is a liberal town. In fact, it is well-documented that right-leaning celebrities are forced into silence or risk being blackballed by the industry. Celebrities are conditioned by agents and publicists on what opinions they should hold. They are not sitting down and reading books or scholarly material in order to formulate political or philosophical opinions for themselves. This explains why they are both uninformed and perfect for mainstream news. They lower the level of discourse in American politics, which is precisely the goal of the press.

The media is actually making Americans dumber, and it is doing so purposefully in the name of ratings, which translate into paychecks. The only requirement to be a political pundit in the mainstream in 2019 is harboring hatred for Trump. That is what left-wing news consumers want to hear, and that is exactly what they are fed. It is the reason 90 percent of the media coverage on Trump is negative.[291]

If the press was not an enemy of ordinary Americans, it would seek to genuinely inform its audience. It would seek to raise the level of public discourse through honest two-sided assessments of relevant issues. But it does not do that. Since left-wingers are the audience of the mainstream press, the press simply panders to them. It offers them irritating bumper-sticker platitudes like "diversity is our strength" that they can repeat at the social justice drum circle while sipping bubble tea and smoking reefer. After all, challenging their leftist worldview would be bad for business. If any of the known left-wing news outlets were to begin providing conservative commentary on issues like abortion, its audience would likely seek out another mainstream press outlet to satisfy its confirmation bias.

That is exactly what happened to neoconservative writer Kevin Williamson, who left his gig at *National Review* to write for *The Atlantic*, a liberal stalwart. Williamson was hired by *The Atlantic* to write conservative opinion columns. *The Atlantic* knew exactly what it was getting when it brought him aboard.

He had been writing conservative think-pieces for years. But after he wrote exactly one conservative column for *The Atlantic*, the public realized that Williamson was pro-life, and the attack dogs were unleashed on him. Far left *Media Matters* dug up a podcast and a Tweet where Williamson likened abortion to murder (not an uncommon or extreme point of view for anyone who is pro-life), and he got canned.[292] *The Atlantic* editor Jeffrey Goldberg explained the firing:

> *The tweet was not merely an impulsive, decontextualized, heat-of-the-moment post, as Kevin had explained it. Furthermore, the language used in the podcast was callous and violent. This runs contrary to The Atlantic's tradition of respectful, well-reasoned debate, and to the values of our workplace. This is not about Kevin's views on abortion. We are striving here to be a big-tent journalism organization at a time of national fracturing. We will continue to build a newsroom that is, as The Atlantic's founding manifesto states, "of no party or clique."*

The Atlantic has no such tradition of "well-reasoned debate." That explanation was obviously a pretext for Williamson's firing over his conservative beliefs. The entirety of the abortion debate centers around whether abortion is, in fact, murder. If *The Atlantic* were interested in any debate at all, it would have applauded Williamson's differing opinion. In reality, it realized that it had little wiggle room with its single-digit IQ audience of social justice numbskulls. If it refused to give Williamson the axe, its readership would simply find leftist content elsewhere. As usual, profit was placed higher on the priority list than honest public discourse, and American media consumers suffered.

The Atlantic is typical of the left-wing press. It does not want to promote open and honest debate. None of the mainstream press outlets do, because that might lead to an informed audience. An informed audience might just start to think on its own. That would be dangerous for the bottom line, considering that, when fully fleshed out, most left-wing ideas are ultimately untenable.

So what are we left with? Brainless commentary from brainless simpletons, translating into a brainless left-wing mob. The social cost of a media apparatus that traffics in blind hatred of a political ideology shared by half the population and feeds its audience imbecilic commentary on a daily basis is surely immense. Only an enemy would seek to purposefully dumb down its following while publicly claiming to do the opposite. It is far easier to take advantage of the ignorant than the well-informed. The press is actively harming America by abolishing thoughtful discourse, and until the left-wing media giants collapse under the weight of their own lies, society will continue to suffer.

CHAPTER 12

THE BOTTOM LINE

In September 2016, Trump pulled off perhaps the most dastardly and hilarious troll ever attempted on the buffoons in the news media. He baited them into gathering at his sparkling new, freshly-opened Trump International Hotel in Washington D.C., for what he told them would be a press conference discussing the Barack Obama "birther" conspiracy. Previously, he had expressed some doubt about whether the 44th president's birth certificate was legitimate, for which the press predictably blasted him. Instead of discussing the conspiracy as advertised, he took the press on a tour of his brand-new property, turning it into a "national infomercial for his latest real estate project," as described resentfully by *Vanity Fair*.[293]

Military veterans, including Medal of Honor recipients, also paraded across the stage to endorse Trump's candidacy while the press waited for him to arrive.

It was a train wreck in slow motion for the media. The cable news stations who had devoted valuable airtime to live coverage of the event could not cut away from the presser while veterans endorsed Trump. That was too disrespectful, even for them. And while he still had their attention, he showed off his fancy new digs in the heart of D.C. on Pennsylvania Avenue. They fumed while ordinary Americans grinned with delight.

"We just got played. We just got played," CNN's John King whined.

"It's hard to imagine this as anything other than a political Rick Roll," Jake Tapper, also of CNN said.

But they simply could not look away, which is sort of a metaphor for the press's existence during the Trump era. He is at the center of nearly every mainstream press story because he hauls in the ratings that allow the news giants to sell advertisements. And business has been booming since Trump rode down the escalator and declared his candidacy for the highest office in the land in June 2015.

Nobody but Trump would have had the nerve to pull a stunt like he did during the grand opening of the Trump International. To regular people who live in places like Missouri and Oklahoma, which mainstream news has snottily dubbed "flyover country," it was pure gold. Those people have been slighted by New York and Los Angeles media elites for decades. They have been called "backwards" and "racist," "bigoted" and "regressive" for half a century by the smug bullies. To them, Trump getting the best of the press was all part of his charm. Trump knew that during his campaign, and he operates on that premise to this day.

When Trump says that the media is the "enemy of the American people," he means just that.

ENEMIES

The press is not Trump's enemy, though it might seem like they are fighting him on a daily basis. But he uses them like a four-dollar whore over and over again, just like he did with the Trump International incident. He crushes them like a bug under his shoe regularly. They cannot possibly hurt him because he operates at such a level that makes him immune to their bullshit.

However, the press can and does hurt ordinary Americans.

So when Trump pushes back against the media, he is fighting them on behalf of you and me, the regular people who do not have the influence that he does. He is standing up to the press on behalf of the "bitter clingers," as Barack Obama once called Christian, gun owning Americans, on behalf of the "basket of deplorables," as Hillary Clinton so kindly labeled 63 million Americans during her second failed presidential campaign, and on behalf of the "dregs of society," as former vice president Joe Biden recently called Trump supporters. Trump is standing between the press and the American people, taking the brunt of the media's blows in protection of those of us who refuse to subscribe to the radical left's agenda.

The media harbors absolute disdain for the ordinary people that make this country go. They are the true opposition party in America, fighting against working class Americans on behalf of the D.C. elite. Without them, the far-left agenda pushed by radicals in D.C. would seem insane to everyone. Because of them, the fringe has gone mainstream. And Trump knows that in order to stop this radical leftist wave in its tracks and protect ordinary Americans, he must go to bat for them against the press.

We now have insurgent socialists like Sen. Bernie Sanders (I-VT), and Rep. Alexandria Ocasio-Cortez (D-NY), supported by millions of brainwashed millennials, most of whom do not believe in capitalism despite the unquestionable fact that socialism has killed millions in the past century.[294] We have drag queens pushing the LGBT agenda on three-year-olds[295] and teachers encouraging kindergartners to change genders,[296] backed by the mainstream press in the name of tolerance and inclusion. We have black-clad masked radicals in the streets committing violent acts against Republicans in the name of fighting imagined fascism, aided and abetted by the press that morally equivocates on their behalf. We have censorship of conservative ideas on social media under the guise of "hate speech," which violates the terms of service conceived by leftist tech giants in Silicon Valley, effectively abolishing the First Amendment.[297] We have leftist politicians promising to abolish Immigration and Customs Enforcement (ICE)[298] in favor of open borders which will inevitably change our nation's culture, as people from all over the world pour into this country unaccounted for and fail to assimilate to our norms. We have calls to abolish the Electoral College so that liberals in New York City and Los Angeles can decide every election from now through eternity.[299]

Mention a word in opposition to any of these decidedly horrible ideas and you will be slandered by the press, pegged as hateful or backwards, and banished from public discourse.

For supporting publicly President Trump or the GOP, you stand a chance of losing your job, your livelihood, or even your Second Amendment right to keep and bear arms, as in the case of Leyla Pirnie. A twenty-four-year-old Harvard graduate student, Pirnie's landlord threw her out for keeping weapons that she legally owned.[300] While Pirnie was away on a weekend trip, her roommates discovered her MAGA hat, which led them to invade her privacy further by entering and searching her room to see what other "unmentionables" they could find. They stumbled across firearms that Pirnie owned for self-defense, and reported her to the landlord because the weapons made them uncomfortable. The landlord was uncomfortable too, and forced Pirnie out.

No one in the mainstream press reported on the egregious violation of a foundational American right.

The media are complicit in, if not actively supportive of, the left's attempt to destroy the very values upon which the America was founded. The leftists in media and their audience believe that this is a fundamentally bad country founded on hatred and bigotry, while normal people, even centrist liberals, recognize that America, while not perfect, was founded upon the finest set of ideas ever conceived by man, and that this is the most prosperous and fair nation ever to grace the earth. The members of the media who have made the conscious decision to peddle the far-left's hatred for America have done so in exchange for whopping paychecks bestowed upon them by their overlords, the corporate media executives. The proverbial bottom line is that Trump-bashing is great for the financial bottom line.

Just ask Jeff Zucker, CNN's chief executive. He makes a cool $6.3 million salary and has a $40 million net worth.[301] He owns a $2.65 million home in the Hamptons and lives in the lap of luxury. Creating division among Americans is Zucker's game. It is how he accrues his wealth.[302]

Consider that Zucker lives lavishly while his network calls ordinary people evil for accepting a small tax break. The "evil" label is the key. If CNN told the truth—that Republicans and Democrats simply disagree on tax policy—Zucker might have to downgrade to a condo in Manhattan. Alarmism, not rational discourse, pays the bills. Divisiveness is a tried and true business model for the media elites. Consequences be damned, they are going to cash their paychecks. He might have to foment an actual civil war to make another million, but Zucker will do it. And his minions will gladly play along.

CNN's star host Anderson Cooper, who anchors "AC 360" in primetime, makes a larger salary than Zucker. Cooper rakes in $12 million per year to bash Trump and the GOP. His net worth is higher than Zucker's, too. He's worth an estimated $110 million.[303] Cooper's mother is an heiress to the wealthy Vanderbilt family, worth billions, but he is self-made. He has not inherited a dime. Instead, he decided to hop on the gravy train of political contentiousness.

Likewise, CNN's Don Lemon, who hosts "CNN Tonight," reportedly makes a cool $1 million per year and has a net worth of $3 million.[304] "Reliable Sources" host Brian Stelter makes an estimated $1 million annually, and has a net worth estimated around $10 million.[305]

MSNBC's primetime host Rachel Maddow makes $7 million annually and has a $20 million net worth.[306] Her colleague Chris Matthews, host of "Hardball," makes $5 million per year, and has an estimated net worth of $16 million.[307] Brian Williams, who left NBC in disgrace after lying about being involved in a helicopter crash while covering the Iraq War, brushed off that incident and eleven others where he was found to have exaggerated the truth while reporting at NBC, for a gig at MSNBC. He makes a solid $10 million salary to host "11th Hour."[308] Not bad for a proven liar. Joe Scarborough, the network's morning show host, makes $99,000 *per week*, which comes out to a salary of $6 million per year. He is worth an estimated $18 million.[309] Scarborough's co-host and newly wedded wife Mika Brzezinski makes an estimated $2 million annually, and has an estimated net worth of $12 million.[310] Together, Scarborough and Brzezinski bring in $8 million per year. The median household income in the United States is $56,516 as of 2015.[311] Annually, the pair earns 106 times more than the ordinary American family that they broadcast to daily. How can any of those people possibly be trusted to inform ordinary Americans when they are so far removed from what it is like to live like an ordinary American?

NBC's Lester Holt earns $4.5 million per year to anchor the nearly-unwatchable "NBC Nightly News." He is worth an estimated $12 million.[312]

Behind every lie about Trump, every smear of Republicans, every disgusting op-ed, every apocalyptic prediction, every hate crime hoax, every awful prediction, every anti-white cable news segment, every omitted fact, every weasel worded "fact-check," and every violent media fantasy of offing Trump, there are dollar signs.

The left-wing press has sold out the values of this county, the rule of law, and any semblance of normalcy in a fit of greed. For that, they have rightfully earned President Trump's designation as enemies of the American people.

ENDNOTES

1   Josh Chapin and Joel Brown, "3 Arrested after Tense Demonstrations near 'Silent Sam' Monument," *ABC11 Raleigh-Durham*, August 31, 2018, accessed December 3, 2018, *https://abc11.com/3-arrested-after-tense-demonstrations-near-silent-sam-monument/4101529/*.

2   Douglas Ernst, "Anti-Trump Protesters Set Muslim Businessman's Limo Ablaze," *The Washington Times*, January 24, 2017, accessed December 10, 2018, *www.washingtontimes.com/news/2017/jan/24/anti-trump-protesters-set-muslim-businessmans-limo/*.

3   Jordan Green, "This New Right-Wing Site Falsely Blamed A UNC Professor For Heather Heyer's Death," *The Huffington Post*, October 21, 2018, accessed December 10, 2018, *www.huffingtonpost.com/entry/big-league-politics-patrick-howley_us_5bbe210de4b0876edaa4a1fd*.

4   Rebecca Riffkin, "Americans' Trust in Media Remains at Historical Low," *Gallup*, 28 September 2015, accessed December 10, 2018, *http://news.gallup.com/poll/185927/americans-trust-media-remains-historical-low.aspx*.

5   Adam Epstein, "Fox News's Biggest Problem Isn't the Ailes Ouster, It's That Its Average Viewer Is a Dinosaur," *Quartz*, July 21, 2016, accessed December 10, 2018, *www.qz.com/738346/fox-newss-biggest-problem-isnt-the-ailes-ouster-its-that-its-average-viewer-is-a-dinosaur/*.

6   Jack Sheperd, "Donald Trump wins: Video of MSNBC host
     Rachel Maddow reminders viewers 'you're not dead' resurfaces,"
     The Independent, November 9, 2016, accessed December 10,
     2018, *www.independent.co.uk/arts-entertainment/tv/news/
     donald-trump-wins-msnbc-rachel-maddow-youre-not-dead-
     dreaming-a7406906.html*.

7   "Cable News Fact Sheet," *Pew Research Center*, June 1,
     2017, accessed December 10, 2018, *www.pewresearch.org/
     wp-content/uploads/sites/8/2018/07/State-of-the-News-
     Media_2017-Archive.pdf#page=7*.

8   Gregory Krieg, "The New Birthers: Debunking the Hillary
     Clinton Health Conspiracy," CNN, August 24, 2016, accessed
     December 10, 2018, *www.cnn.com/2016/08/22/politics/hillary-
     clinton-health-conspiracy-theory-explained/index.html*.

9   Matt Wilstein, "2014 Cable News Ratings: CNN Beats MSNBC
     in Primetime Demo, Fox Still #1," *MEDIAite*, December
     30, 2014, accessed December 10, 2018, *www.mediaite.com/
     tv/2014-cable-news-ratings-cnn-beats-msnbc-in-primetime-
     demo-fox-still-1/*.

10   Brian Flood, "2015 Ratings: CNN Up Big In Prime
     Time and Key Demo," *Adweek*, December 30, 2015,
     accessed December 10, 2018, *www.adweek.com/
     tvnewser/2015-ratings-cnn-up-big-after-dismal-2014/280727*.

11   A. J. Katz, "2016 Ratings: CNN Has Most-Watched
     Year Ever," *Adweek*, December 28, 2016, accessed
     December 10, 2018, *https://www.adweek.com/
     tvnewser/2016-ratings-cnn-has-most-watched-year-ever/315014*.

12 A. J. Katz, "2017 Ratings: CNN Has Its Largest Audience Ever, But Sees Prime Time Losses," *Adweek*, December 27, 2017, accessed December 10, 2018, *https://www.adweek.com/tvnewser/2017-ratings-cnn-is-down-in-prime-time-but-earns-its-largest-audience-ever-in-total-day/353147.*

13 A. J. Katz, "Q3 2018 Ratings: 10 P.M. Hour of CNN Tonight with Don Lemon Has Its Highest-Rated Quarter on Record," *Adweek*, October 2, 2018, accessed December 10, 2018, *https://www.adweek.com/tvnewser/q3-2018-ratings-cnn-tonight-with-don-lemon-has-its-highest-rated-quarter-on-record/378269.*

14 Sally Peck, "Al Gore's 'nine Inconvenient Untruths,'" *The Telegraph*, October 11, 2007, accessed December 12, 2018, *https://www.telegraph.co.uk/news/earth/earthnews/3310137/Al-Gores-nine-Inconvenient-Untruths.html.*

15 "An Inconvenient Truth," *Box Office Mojo*, accessed December 12, 2018, *https://www.boxofficemojo.com/movies/?id=inconvenienttruth.htm.*

16 "Roy W. Spencer," *DESMOG*, accessed December 12, 2018, *https://www.desmogblog.com/roy-spencer.*

17 Steve Benen, "Some NC Republicans Rethink the Value of Denying Climate Change," *MSNBC*, October 19, 2018, accessed December 12, 2018, *http://www.msnbc.com/rachel-maddow-show/some-nc-republicans-rethink-the-value-denying-climate-change.*

18 John Abraham, "Victims of Hurricane Michael Are Represented by Climate Deniers," *The Guardian*, October 11, 2018, accessed December 12, 2018, *https://www.theguardian.com/environment/climate-consensus-97-per-cent/2018/oct/11/victims-of-hurricane-michael-voted-for-climate-deniers.*

19   Nicholas Kristof, "The 'Greatest Hoax' Strikes Florida," *The New York Times*, October 10, 2018, accessed December 12, 2018, *https://www.nytimes.com/2018/10/10/opinion/climate-change-hurricane-michael.html*.

20   Robinson Meyer, "Syria Is Joining the Paris Agreement. Now What?" *The Atlantic*, November 8, 2017, accessed December 12, 2018, *https://www.theatlantic.com/science/archive/2017/11/syria-is-joining-the-paris-agreement-now-what/545261/*.

21   "Thousands Face Starvation in Syrian Desert Camp," *The Straits Times*, November 2, 2018, accessed December 12, 2018, *https://www.straitstimes.com/world/middle-east/thousands-face-starvation-in-syrian-desert-camp*.

22   Ben Hubbard, "'There Are No Girls Left': Syria's Christian Villages Hollowed Out by ISIS," *The New York Times*, August 15, 2018, accessed December 12, 2018, *https://www.nytimes.com/2018/08/15/world/middleeast/syria-isis-assyrian-christians.html*.

23   Oren Cass, "We'll Never Have Paris," *City Journal*, June 1, 2017, accessed December 12, 2018, *https://www.city-journal.org/html/well-never-have-paris-15231.html*.

24   Jeff Cox, "Economist Larry Summers Predicts 10,000 Will Die per Year Due to Tax Reform," *CNBC*, December 4, 2017, accessed December 12, 2018, *https://www.cnbc.com/2017/12/04/economist-larry-summers-10000-will-die-per-year-due-to-tax-reform.html?__source=twitter%7Cmain*.

25   Jack McCarthy, "OIG: 300,000 Vets Died Waiting for Care," *Healthcare IT News*, September 4, 2015, accessed

December 12, 2018, *https://www.healthcareitnews.com/news/ oig-300000-vets-died-waiting-care*.

26   "MSNBC Guest Says Republican Tax Bill Is 'Akin to Rape,'" interview with Bruce Bartlett by Joy Ann Reid on MSNBC, December 4, 2017, accessed December 12, 2018, video, 1:12, *https://www.youtube.com/ watch?time_continue=72&v=j1cfteKtyc*.

27   Cristina Marcos, "Pelosi: GOP Tax Proposal 'the Worst Bill in the History' of Congress," *The Hill*, December 4, 2017, accessed December 13, 2018, *https://thehill.com/blogs/floor-action/ house/363240-pelosi-gop-tax-proposal-the-worst-bill-in-the- history-of-the-united*.

28   Brian Riedl, "Looking Back at the Democratic Hysteria Over Trump's Tax Cuts," *The Weekly Standard*, March 29, 2018, accessed December 12, 2018, *https://www.weeklystandard.com/brian-riedl/ looking-back-at-the-democratic-hysteria-over-trumps-tax-cuts*.

29   Catherine Rampell, "Apparently Republicans Want to Kick the Middle Class in the Face," *The Washington Post*, November 30, 2017, accessed December 12, 2018, *https:// www.washingtonpost.com/opinions/apparently-republi- cans-want-to-kick-the-middle-class-in-the-face/2017/11/30/ ab0e4e9a-d616-11e7-a986-d0a9770d9a3e_story. html?utm_term=.99bea43ff234*.

30   Robert S. McElvaine, "I'm a Depression Historian. The GOP Tax Bill Is Straight out of 1929," *The Washington Post*, November 30, 2017, accessed December 12, 2018, *https://www. washingtonpost.com/news/posteverything/wp/2017/11/30/ im-a-depression-historian-the-gop-tax-bill-is-straight-out-of- 1929/?utm_term=.d8877090955a*.

31   Douglas Ernst, "Nancy Pelosi Scoffs at 'crumb' Bonuses
       by U.S. Companies as a Result of Tax Cuts," *The Wash-
       ington Times*, January 11, 2018, accessed December 12,
       2018, *https://www.washingtontimes.com/news/2018/jan/11/
       nancy-pelosi-scoffs-at-crumb-bonuses-by-us-compani/*.

32   Scott Greenberg, "Summary of the Latest Federal Income
       Tax Data, 2016 Update," Tax Foundation, February 1, 2017,
       accessed December 12, 2018, *https://taxfoundation.org/
       summary-latest-federal-income-tax-data-2016-update/*.

33   Yuval Rosenberg, "Heritage Foundation: Average House-
       hold in Every State Will Get a Tax Cut in 2018," *The Fiscal
       Times*, July 23, 2018, accessed December 12, 2018, *http://www.
       thefiscaltimes.com/2018/07/23/Heritage-Foundation-Average-
       Household-Every-State-Will-Get-Tax-Cut-2018*.

34   Paul Krugman, "Republicans' Tax Lies Show the Rot Spreads
       Wide and Runs Deep," *The New York Times*, November
       30, 2017, accessed January 16, 2019, *https://www.nytimes.
       com/2017/11/30/opinion/republican-tax-lies-fed.html*

35   Nicholas Jasinski, "Stock Swoon? What Stock Swoon?
       Consumer Confidence Up," *Barron's*, November 2, 2018,
       accessed December 12, 2018, *https://www.barrons.com/articles/
       consumer-confidence-hits-17-year-high-1541203480*.

36   Jordyn Phelps and Conor Finnegan, "President Trump Says
       He Wants to Pull Troops out of Syria," *ABC News*, April 3, 2018,
       accessed December 12, 2018, *https://abcnews.go.com/Politics/
       president-trump-pull-troops-syria/story?id=54208786*.

37   Jackson Diehl, "Trump May Not Intend to Start a War. But He
       Sure Could Bumble into One," *The Washington Post*, April 1,

2018, accessed December 12, 2018, *https://www.washingtonpost. com/opinions/global-opinions/trump-may-not-intend-to-start-a-war-but-he-sure-could-bumble-into-one/2018/04/01/2710ac22-335f-11e8-8bdd-cdb33a5eef83_story.html.*

38   Jeremy Page, Andrew Jeong, and Ian Talley, "China, Finally, Clamps Down on North Korea Trade—And the Impact Is Stinging," *The Wall Street Journal*, March 2, 2018, accessed December 12, 2018, *https://www.wsj.com/articles/north-korea-finally-feels-the-sting-of-international-sanctions-1519923280.*

39   Ciaran McGrath, "Trump 'has No Conception of the Risk of Nuclear War', Warn Experts," *Express*, July 28, 2018, accessed December 12, 2018, *https://www.express.co.uk/news/world/995161/ trump-nuclear-war-risk-iran-cuban-missile-crisis-russia.*

40   Jeffrey Lewis, "How Trump Could Trigger Armageddon With a Tweet," *Wired*, September 5, 2018, accessed December 12, 2018, *https://www.wired.com/story/ how-trump-could-trigger-armageddon-with-a-tweet/.*

41   Jeffrey Lewis, "This Is How Nuclear War with North Korea Would Unfold – Step by Step," *The Independent*, January 29, 2018, accessed December 12, 2018, *https://www.independent. co.uk/news/long_reads/north-korea-nuclear-war-how-it-happen-us-twitter-donald-trump-reaction-a8173391.html.*

42   "NO MORE MR. WHITE GUY," *Ann Coulter*, September 26, 2018, accessed December 11, 2018, *http://www.anncoulter.com/ columns/2018-09-26.html.*

43   Peter D'Abrosca, "Hawaiian Senator: Men Should 'Shut Up' And 'Do The Right Thing For A Change' in Kavanaugh

Case," *Big League Politics*, September 19, 2018, accessed December 11, 2018, *https://bigleaguepolitics.com/hawaiian-senator-men-should-shut-up-and-do-the-right-thing-for-a-change-in-kavanaugh-case/*.

44   Patricia Murphy, "Don't Call Mazie Hirono a Badass. Call Her a Leader," *Roll Call*, September 25, 2018, accessed December 11, 2018, *https://www.rollcall.com/news/opinion/dont-call-her-badass-call-her-leader*.

45   Peter D'Abrosca, "Lindsey Graham Fires Back At Sexist Mazie Hirono: 'I Will Not Shut Up'" *Big League Politics*, September 29, 2018, accessed December 11, 2018, *https://bigleaguepolitics.com/lindsey-graham-fires-back-at-sexist-mazie-hirono-i-will-not-shut-up/*.

46   Jonathan Capehart, "Hell Hath No Fury like an Entitled White Man Denied," *The Washington Post*, September 28, 2018, accessed December 11, 2018, *https://www.washingtonpost.com/blogs/post-partisan/wp/2018/09/28/im-not-here-for-the-entitlement-of-kavanaugh-and-graham/?utm_term=.d3640d1cd24a*.

47   Erika D. Smith, "A Crying Brett Kavanaugh. This Is What White Male Privilege Looks like," *The Sacramento Bee*, September 27, 2018, accessed December 11, 2018, *https://www.sacbee.com/opinion/opn-columns-blogs/erika-d-smith/article219146885.html*.

48   Matthew Dowd, "Us White Male Christians Need to Step Back and Give Others Room to Lead: OPINION," *ABC News*, September 30, 2018, accessed December 11, 2018, *https://abcnews.go.com/US/leadership-means-making-oneself-dispensable-opinion/story?id=58193412*.

49   Pete Forester (@pete_forester), "I HATE WHITE PEOPLE,"
      Twitter Tweet, April 16, 2018, accessed December 11, 2018,
      http://archive.fo/DtxRo.

50   Ben Howe (@BenHowe), "@GeraldoRivera yeah. White people
      are stupid," Twitter Tweet, June 28, 2013, accessed December 11,
      2018, *http://archive.fo/Vv0mv.*

51   Catherine Deveny (@CatherineDeveny), "white people suck,"
      Twitter Tweet, January 18, 2018, accessed December 11, 2018,
      http://archive.fo/shlij.

52   Christina Warren (@film_girl), "Fuck white people," Twitter
      Tweet, November 8, 2016, accessed December 11, 2018, *http://
      archive.fo/3UVhH.*

53   Dan Arel (@danarel), "we Need white genocide more than ever,"
      Twitter Tweet, June 16, 2017, accessed December 11, 2018, *http://
      archive.fo/rFiqV.*

54   Peter D'Abrosca, "'White Men Are Bull****': *New York Times*
      Hires Openly Anti-White Racist Editor," *Big League Poli-
      tics*, August 02, 2018, accessed December 11, 2018, *https://
      bigleaguepolitics.com/white-men-are-bull-new-york-times-
      hires-openly-anti-white-racist-editor/.*

55   Peter D'Abrosca, "*New York Times* Blames Racism for New
      Editor's Racism," *Big League Politics*, August 03, 2018,
      accessed December 11, 2018, *https://bigleaguepolitics.com/
      new-york-times-blames-racism-for-new-editors-racism/.*

56   Amber Athey, "Georgetown Professor: 'Castrate' White Men's
      Corpses And 'Feed Them To Swine,'" *The Daily Caller*, October
      1, 2018, accessed December 11, 2018, *https://dailycaller.
      com/2018/10/01/georgetown-christine-fair-white-men-swine/.*

57   Jack Crosbie, "Tucker Carlson's Racist Dog Whistle of the
      Night Is White 'Genocide,'" Splinter, October 1, 201, accessed
      December 11, 2018, *https://splinternews.com/tucker-carl-
      sons-racist-dog-whistle-of-the-night-is-whit-1829454231*.

58   Manisha Krishnan, "Dear White People, Please Stop Pretending
      Reverse Racism Is Real," *Vice*, October 2, 2016, accessed
      December 11, 2018, *https://www.vice.com/en_us/article/kwzjvz/
      dear-white-people-please-stop-pretending-reverse-racism-is-real*.

59   George Yancy, "Dear White America," *The New York Times*,
      December 24, 2015, accessed December 11, 2018, *https://opin-
      ionator.blogs.nytimes.com/2015/12/24/dear-white-america/*.

60   Lydia O'Connor and Daniel Marans, "Here Are 13 Examples
      Of Donald Trump Being Racist," *The Huffington Post*,
      February 29, 2016, accessed December 11, 2018, *https://www.
      huffingtonpost.com/entry/donald-trump-racist-examples_
      us_56d47177e4b03260bf777e83*.

61   Megan Tremble, "KKK Groups Still Active in These
      States in 2017," *U.S. News & World Report*, August
      14, 2017, accessed December 11, 2018, *https://www.
      usnews.com/news/best-states/articles/2017-08-14/
      the-kkk-is-still-based-in-22-states-in-the-us-in-2017*.

62   "Survey: Americans Forget National Anthem," *ABC News*, May
      20, 2004, accessed December 11, 2018, *https://abcnews.go.com/
      GMA/story?id=124484*.

63   "Americans Are Poorly Informed About Basic Constitutional
      Provisions," *Annenberg Public Policy Center of the Univer-
      sity of Pennsylvania*, September 12, 2017, accessed December
      11, 2018, *https://www.annenbergpublicpolicycenter.org/*

americans-are-poorly-informed-about-basic-constitutional-provisions/.

64   Lydia O'Connor and Daniel Marans, "Here Are 16 Examples Of Donald Trump Being Racist," *The Huffington Post,* December 13, 2016, accessed December 11, 2018, *https://www.huffingtonpost.com/entry/president-donald-trump-racist-examples_us_584f2ccae4b0bd9c3dfe5566.*

65   Robert Barnes and Ann E. Marimow, "Supreme Court Upholds Trump Travel Ban," *The Washington Post,* June 26, 2018, accessed December 11, 2018, *https://www.washingtonpost.com/politics/courts_law/supreme-court-upholds-trump-travel-ban/2018/06/26/b79cb09a-7943-11e8-80be-6d32e182a3bc_story.html?utm_term=.6cb39392a4f8.*

66   Robert Parry, "Is Mitt Romney a Racist?" *Consortium News,* August 25, 2012, accessed December 11, 2018, *https://consortiumnews.com/2012/08/25/is-mitt-romney-a-racist/.*

67   Lola Adesioye, "Palling Around With Racists," *The Guardian,* October 14, 2008, accessed December 11, 2018, *https://www.theguardian.com/commentisfree/cifamerica/2008/oct/14/mccain-palin-obama-racism.*

68   Nicholas Kristof, "John McCain, a Maverick We Can Learn From," *The New York Times,* August 25, 2018, accessed December 11, 2018, *https://www.nytimes.com/2018/08/25/opinion/john-mccain-death.html.*

69   Kurt Schlichter, "The Only Good Republican Is A Dead Republican," *Townhall,* December 3, 2018, accessed December 11, 2018, *https://townhall.com/columnists/kurtschlichter/2018/12/03/the-only-good-republican-is-a-dead-republican-n2536850.*

70   Bill Scher, "Newsflash: It's Going To Be Hillary vs. Jeb," *POLITICO*, May 31, 2015, accessed December 11, 2018, *https://www.politico.com/magazine/story/2015/05/2016-hillary-vs-jeb-118466*.

71   Karen Tumulty and Matea Gold, "Jeb Bush Has Become the GOP Front-runner for 2016 – so Now What?" *The Washington Post*, January 31, 2015, accessed December 11, 2018, *https://www.washingtonpost.com/politics/jeb-bush-has-become-the-gop-front-runner-for-2016--so-now-what/2015/01/31/0105ca68-a96e-11e4-a06b-9df2002b86a0_story.html?utm_term=.cd7686ca8121*.

72   Nate Silver, "What Went Down In The March 8 Presidential Primaries," *FiveThirtyEight*, March 09, 2016, accessed December 11, 2018, *https://fivethirtyeight.com/live-blog/michigan-mississippi-idaho-hawaii-primaries-presidential-election-2016/#livepress-update-20072287*.

73   "State Delegations Vote During the Roll Call of States," Clip of Democratic National Convention, Day 2 on C-SPAN, July 26, 2016, accessed December 11, 2018, video, 1:31:25, *https://www.c-span.org/video/?c4615252%2Fstate-delegations-vote-roll-call-states*.

74   Bill Kristol (@BillKristol), "Just a heads up over this holiday weekend: There will be an independent candidate--an impressive one, with a strong team and a real chance," Twitter Tweet, May 29, 2016, accessed December 11, 2018, *http://archive.is/VCbMo*.

75   "The Republicans Opposing Donald Trump – And Voting for Hillary Clinton," *NBC News*, November 6, 2016, accessed December 11, 2018,

*https://www.nbcnews.com/politics/2016-election/
meet-republicans-speaking-out-against-trump-n530696.*

76   "Keith Olbermann on 'The View': Says Republican Party Will
Stop Trump from Getting Nomination," interview with Keith
Olbermann on The View, March 25, 2016, accessed December
11, 2018, video, 5:04, *https://abc.go.com/playlists/PL552614593/
video/VDKA0_rj2i31ma.*

77   Joe Concha, "Keith Olbermann: 'I Am Retiring from Political Commentary,'" *The Hill*, November 27, 2017, accessed
December 11, 2018, *https://thehill.com/homenews/
media/362068-keith-olbermann-i-am-retiring-from-politi-
cal-commentary.*

78   "Real Time with Bill Maher: Overtime – June 19, 2015 (HBO),"
interview with Ann Coulter by Bill Maher on Real Time with
Bill Maher, June 19, 2015, accessed December 11, 2018, video,
9:02, *https://www.youtube.com/watch?v=0-2uSG1xUEg.*

79   "Who Will Win the Presidency," *FiveThirtyEight*, November
08, 2016, accessed December 11, 2018, *https://projects.fivethir-
tyeight.com/2016-election-forecast/.*

80   Natalie Jackson and Adam Hooper, "Forecast PRESIDENT
SENATE," *The Huffington Post*, October 3, 2016, accessed
December 10, 2018, *https://elections.huffingtonpost.com/2016/
forecast/president.*

81   "RECALLED NEWSWEEK MADAM PRESIDENT HILLARY
CLINTON MAGAZINE COMMEMORATIVE EDITION,"
EBay, accessed December 11, 2018, *https://www.ebay.com/
itm/RECALLED-NEWSWEEK-MADAM-PRESIDENT-HIL-
LARY-CLINTON-MAGAZINE-COMMEMORATIVE-EDITION
-/253824769664?oid=202492283880.*

82   "Some Thoughts On Pretending And Honesty," Stephen
      Colbert on The Late Show with Stephen Colbert, October 3,
      2015, accessed December 11, 2018, video, 7:58, *https://www.
      youtube.com/watch?v=Brg5ChOTaZM.*

83   David Rutz, "Democrats and Media Agreed: There Was No
      Way Trump Could Get Elected President," *The Washington
      Free Beacon*, November 10, 2016, accessed December 11, 2018,
      *https://freebeacon.com/politics/democrats-and-media-agreed-
      there-was-no-way-donald-trump-could-get-elected-president/.*

84   "Bob Beckel: This Race, Effectively, As Of Tonight, Is Over,"
      interview with Bob Beckel on CNN, October 7, 2016, accessed
      December 11, 2018, video, 00:53, *https://www.realclearpolitics.
      com/video/2016/10/07/bob_beckel_this_election_is_over.html.*

85   "CNN Tonight With Don Lemon," interview with Hilary Rosen
      by Don Lemon on CNN Tonight, November 7, 2016, accessed
      December 11, 2018, video, 1:02, *https://archive.org/details/
      CNNW_20161108_030000_CNN_Tonight_With_Don_Lemon/
      start/2880/end/2940.*

86   Kurt Eichenwald (@kurteichenwald) "In preparation for a
      completely unpredictable Trump..." Twitter Tweet, September
      26, 2016, accessed December 11, 2018, *http://archive.is/vWfvz.*

87   Joe Concha, "Vanity Fair Distances Itself from Kurt Eichenwald
      after Journalist Launches Attack on Parkland Student," *The
      Hill*, April 3, 2018, accessed December 11, 2018, *https://thehill.
      com/homenews/media/381519-vanity-fair-distances-itself-from-
      kurt-eichenwald-after-journalist-launches.*

88   Paul Farhi, "A Reporter Tweets His Way into Trouble
      with a Claim about Trump That Lacked Evidence,"

The Washington Post, September 14, 2016, accessed December 11, 2018, *https://www.washingtonpost.com/ lifestyle/style/a-reporter-tweets-his-way-into-trouble-with-a-claim-about-trump-that-lacked-evidence/2016/09/14/ f8bd2a54-7a95-11e6-beac-57a4a412e93a_story.html?utm_ term=.bf1bba07aa21.*

89   John Ridley, "Sex, Checks and '*The New York Times*,'" *NPR*, August 15, 2007, accessed December 13, 2018, *https://www.npr. org/sections/visibleman/2007/08/sex_checks_and_the_new_ york_ti_1.html.*

90   Ben White, "Economists: A Trump Win Would Tank the Markets," *POLITICO*, October 21, 2016, accessed December 11, 2018, *https://www.politico.com/story/2016/10/ donald-trump-wall-street-effect-markets-230164.*

91   "A President Trump Could Destroy the World Economy," *The Washington Post*, October 05, 2016, accessed December 11, 2018, *https://www.washingtonpost.com/opinions/a-pres- ident-trump-could-destroy-the-world-economy/2016/10/05/ f70019c0-84df-11e6-92c2-14b64f3d453f_story.html?utm_term=. cf9bd0325e8f.*

92   Drew DeSilver, "For Most Americans, Real Wages Have Barely Budged for Decades," *Pew Research Center*, August 07, 2018, accessed December 11, 2018, *http://www.pewresearch.org/ fact-tank/2018/08/07/for-most-us-workers-real-wages-have- barely-budged-for-decades/.*

93   Paul Krugman, "Paul Krugman: The Economic Fallout," *The New York Times*, November 9, 2016, accessed December 11, 2018, *https://www.nytimes.com/inter- active/projects/cp/opinion/election-night-2016/ paul-krugman-the-economic-fallout.*

94 Tom Teodorczuk, "Michael Moore Predicts Trump-driven Economic Crash and Advises Not to Invest in Stock Market," *MarketWatch*, August 16, 2017, accessed December 11, 2018, *https://www.marketwatch.com/story/michael-moore-predicts-trump-driven-economic-crash-and-advises-not-to-invest-in-stock-market-2017-08-11*.

95 Heather Long, "Unemployment Rate Falls to 3.7 Percent, Lowest since 1969," *The Washington Post*, October 05, 2018, accessed December 11, 2018, *https://www.washingtonpost.com/business/2018/10/05/unemployment-rate-falls-percent-lowest-since/?noredirect=on&utm_term=.a5544294f451*.

96 Catherine Clifford, "Small-business Owners Report Pay over $83,000 in Regulatory Costs in the First Year, New Survey Shows," *CNBC*, January 18, 2017, accessed December 11, 2018, *https://www.cnbc.com/2017/01/17/small-business-owners-pay-over-83000-dollars-in-regulatory-costs-in-first-year.html*.

97 Terry Jones, "Deregulation Nation: President Trump Cuts Regulations At Record Rate," *Investor's Business Daily*, August 14, 2018, accessed December 11, 2018, *https://www.investors.com/politics/commentary/deregulation-nation-president-trump-cuts-regulations-at-record-rate/*.

98 P.R. Lockhart, "The Black Unemployment Rate Just Hit a Record Low, but There's a Catch," *Vox*, June 1, 2018, accessed December 11, 2018, *https://www.vox.com/policy-and-politics/2018/6/1/17417762/black-unemployment-rate-record-low-may-jobs-report*.

99 Bannister Craig, "Hispanic-Latino Unemployment Rate Hits Lowest Level on Record in June," *CNS News*, July 6, 2018, accessed December 11, 2018, *https://www.cnsnews.com/*

news/article/craig-bannister/hispanic-latino-unemploy-ment-rate-hits-lowest-level-record-june.

100 Zack Stanton and Derek Robertson, "The Worst Political Predictions of 2017," *POLITICO*, December 27, 2017, accessed December 11, 2018, *https://www.politico.com/magazine/ story/2017/12/27/worst-predictions-2017-trump-politics-216170.*

101 Randall Schweller, "Three Cheers for Trump's Foreign Policy," *Foreign Affairs*, essay, September/October 2018 issue, accessed December 11, 2018, *https://www.foreignaffairs.com/articles/ world/2018-08-13/three-cheers-trumps-foreign-policy.*

102 Tony Schwartz (@tonyschwartz), "I still believe (and pray) Trump will resign by year..." Twitter Tweet, October 12, 2017, accessed December 11, 2018, *http://archive.is/ynsb0.*

103 "PREDICTION: Trump Will Resign In Disgrace...Soon," Cenk Uygur on The Young Turks, August 16, 2017, accessed December 11, 2018, video, 10:49, *https://www.youtube.com/ watch?v=ScgVbT_fry0&vl=en.*

104 Joanna Walters, "'Trump's Going to Be Forced to Resign': Stormy Daniels' Lawyer Predicts a Fall," *The Guardian*, May 6, 2018, accessed December 12, 2018, *https://www.theguardian.com/us-news/2018/may/06/ stormy-daniels-lawyer-michael-avenatti-donald-trump.*

105 Amanda Arnold, and Opheli Garcia Lawler, "What We Know About Michael Avenatti's Arrest for Domestic Violence," *The Cut*, November 21, 2018, accessed December 12, 2018, *https:// www.thecut.com/2018/11/michael-avenatti-arrested-for-domestic-violence.html.*

106 Christal Hayes, "Stormy Daniels Says Avenatti Filed Defamation Suit against Trump 'against My Wishes,'" *USA Today*, November 28, 2018, accessed December 12, 2018, *https://www.usatoday.com/story/news/politics/2018/11/28/stormy-daniels-michael-avenatti-filed-trump-suit-without-permission/2144443002/*.

107 Peter D'Abrosca, "STORMY: Avenatti Hiding Crowdfunded Cash From Me!" *Big League Politics*, November 28, 2018, accessed December 12, 2018, *https://bigleaguepolitics.com/avenatti-responds-stormys-claim-that-hes-hiding-crowdfunded-cash-from-her/*

108 Courtney Sender, "He Asked Permission to Touch, but Not to Ghost," *The New York Times*, September 7, 2018, accessed December 10, 2018, *https://www.nytimes.com/2018/09/07/style/modern-love-he-asked-permission-to-touch-but-not-to-ghost.html*.

109 Ross Douthat, "The Redistribution of Sex," *The New York Times*, May 2, 2018, accessed December 10, 2018, *https://www.nytimes.com/2018/05/02/opinion/incels-sex-robots-redistribution.html*.

110 Moira Donegan, "Actually We Don't Owe You Sex, and We Never Will," *Cosmopolitan*, May 04, 2018, accessed December 10, 2018, *https://www.cosmopolitan.com/politics/a20138446/redistribution-sex-incels/*.

111 Andrea Long Chu, "My New Vagina Won't Make Me Happy," *The New York Times*, November 24, 2018, accessed December 10, 2018, https://www.nytimes.com/2018/11/24/opinion/sunday/vaginoplasty-transgender-medicine.html.\

112   Brittany Wong, "What It's Like To Date When You're Asexual," *The Huffington Post*, November 12, 2018, accessed December 10, 2018, *https://www.huffpost.com/entry/ dating-when-youre-asexual_n_5be4d00ae4b0dbe871a8efda.*

113   Alexa Tsoulis-Reay, "What It's Like to Date a Horse," *New York Magazine*, November 20, 2014, accessed December 10, 2018, *http://nymag.com/scienceofus/2014/11/what-its-like-to-date-a-horse.html.*

114   Maggie Haberman, Glenn Thrush, and Peter Baker, "Inside Trump's Hour-by-Hour Battle for Self-Preservation," *The New York Times*, December 9, 2017, accessed December 10, 2018, *https://www.nytimes.com/2017/12/09/ us/politics/donald-trump-president.html?mtrref=t. co&gwh=E351F789F5E14843978804A049B39047&gwt=pay.*

115   "Stormy Daniels," IMDb, accessed December 10, 2018, *https:// www.imdb.com/name/nm1317917/.*

116   Chris Riotta, "Stormy Daniels Defamation Case against Trump Set to Be Dismissed, Judge Signals," *The Independent*, September 25, 2018, accessed December 10, 2018, *https:// www.independent.co.uk/news/world/americas/us-politics/ stormy-daniels-donald-trump-lawsuit-tweet-con-job-twitter-james-otero-charles-porn-star-harder-a8554311.html.*

117   Tom McCarthy, "Stormy Daniels' Tell-all Book on Trump: Salacious Detail and Claims of Cheating," *The Guardian*, September 18, 2018, accessed December 10, 2018, *https://www. theguardian.com/us-news/2018/sep/18/stormy-daniels-tell-all-book-on-trump-salacious-detail-and-claims-of-cheating.*

118 Geoffrey Dickens and Bill D'Agostino, "Judge to
     Porn Star's Lawyer: Stop Your 'Publicity Tour' (Now
     at 162 Interviews)," MRC *NewsBusters*, May 31, 2018,
     accessed December 10, 2018, *https://www.news-
     busters.org/blogs/nb/geoffrey-dickens/2018/05/31/
     judge-porn-stars-lawyer-stop-your-publicity-tour.*

119 "Tucker and Avenatti Trade Blows in Explosive Interview,"
     interview with Michael Avenatti by Tucker Carlson on Fox
     News, September 13, 2018, accessed December 10, 2018, video,
     13:26, *https://www.youtube.com/watch?v=fxjOEbvdDc8.*

120 Davide Rutz, "CNN, MSNBC Have given Stormy
     Daniels Lawyer Michael Avenatti $175 Million in Earned
     Media," *Fox News*, May 11, 2018, accessed December
     10, 2018, *http://www.foxnews.com/politics/2018/05/11/
     cnn-msnbc-have-given-stormy-daniels-lawyer-michael-avenat-
     ti-175-million-in-earned-media.html.*

121 "Presidential Approval Ratings -- Donald Trump," *Gallup*,
     accessed December 10, 2018, *https://news.gallup.com/
     poll/203198/presidential-approval-ratings-donald-trump.aspx.*

122 Joshua Caplan, "Report: Prosecutor Rachel Mitchell 'Would
     Not Charge Kavanaugh or Even Pursue a Search Warrant,'"
     Breitbart, September 28, 2018, accessed December 10, 2018,
     *https://www.breitbart.com/big-government/2018/09/28/
     report-prosecutor-rachel-mitchell-would-not-charge-kavana-
     ugh-or-even-pursue-a-search-warrant/.*

123 Patrick Howley, "PHONE AUDIO: CNN Producer Cold
     – Calling Brett Kavanaugh's Yale Classmates," *Big League Poli-
     tics*, September 24, 2018, accessed December 10, 2018, *https://
     bigleaguepolitics.com/phone-audio-cnn-producer-cold-calling-
     brett-kavanaughs-yale-classmates/.*

124 Ronan Farrow and Jane Mayer, "A Sexual-Misconduct Allegation Against the Supreme Court Nominee Brett Kavanaugh Stirs Tension Among Democrats in Congress," *The New Yorker*, September 14, 2018, accessed December 10, 2018, *https://www.newyorker.com/news/news-desk/a-sexual-misconduct-allegation-against-the-supreme-court-nominee-brett-kavanaugh-stirs-tension-among-democrats-in-congress*.

125 "I Am Part of the Resistance Inside the Trump Administration," *The New York Times*, September 05, 2018, accessed December 10, 2018, *https://www.nytimes.com/2018/09/05/opinion/trump-white-house-anonymous-resistance.html*.

126 Jessica Estepa, "Third Woman Makes Sexual Misconduct Allegations about Supreme Court Nominee Brett Kavanaugh," *USA Today*, September 26, 2018, accessed December 10, 2018, *https://www.usatoday.com/story/news/politics/2018/09/26/brett-kavanaugh-confirmation-michael-avenatti-julie-swetnick/1431133002/*.

127 Geoff Earle, "Michael Avenatti Says a Third Woman will 'Literally Risk Her Life' to Come Forward and Accuse SCOTUS Nominee Kavanaugh of Sexual Misconduct Within the Next 48 Hours and Teases 'Criminal Charges,'" *Daily Mail*, September 24, 2018, accessed December 11, 2018, *https://www.dailymail.co.uk/news/article-6204023/Michael-Avenatti-says-woman-come-forward-Wednesday-accuse-Kavanaugh-misconduct.html*.

128 "TRANSCRIPTS, Cuomo Primetime," CNN, 24 September 2018, accessed February 5, 2019, *http://transcripts.cnn.com/TRANSCRIPTS/1809/24/CPT.01.html*

129 "RADIO CLIPS, The Glenn Beck Program," *glenn*, November 21, 2008, accessed December 12, 2018, *https://www.glennbeck. com/content/articles/article/198/18490/*.

130 "Fake Hate Crimes: A Database of Hate Crime Hoaxes in the USA," Fakehatecrimes.org, accessed December 12, 2018, *http:// www.fakehatecrimes.org/*.

131 Elissa Strauss, "The JCC Bomb Threats Confirm That Jewish Parents Are Right to Be Afraid," *Slate Magazine*, January 19, 2017, accessed December 12, 2018, *https://slate. com/human-interest/2017/01/the-jcc-bomb-threats-confirm-that-jewish-parents-are-right-to-be-afraid.html*.

132 AnneClaire Stapleton and Eric Levenson, "Jewish Center Bomb Threats Top 100; Kids Pulled from Schools," CNN, March 13, 2017, accessed December 12, 2018, *https://www.cnn.com/2017/02/28/ us/bomb-threats-jewish-centers-jcc/index.html*.

133 Bar Peleg,"Israeli-American Who Terrorized U.S. Jews with Thousands of Bomb Threats Jailed for 10 Years," *Haaretz*, November 22, 2018, accessed December 12, 2018, *https://www. haaretz.com/israel-news/israeli-american-hacker-who-terror-ized-u-s-jews-with-bomb-threats-gets-10-years-1.6677435*.

134 Kate Smith, "Arrest Made in Anti-Semitic Graffiti at Brooklyn Synagogue That Led to Event Cancellation," *CBS News*, November 02, 2018, accessed December 12, 2018, *https://www. cbsnews.com/news/anti-semitic-vandalism-brooklyn-can-cels-ilana-glazer-political-event/*.

135 Dean Obiedallah (@DeanObeidallah), "This happened last night in NYC- this is..." Twitter Tweet, November 2, 2018, accessed December 12, 2018, *http://archive.is/IcLV8*.

136   Lesley Abravanel (@lesleyabravanel), "This week in NYC:…"
       November 3, 2018, accessed December 12, 2018, *http://archive.*
       is/wgwtq.

137   Dom Calicchio, "Synagogue Vandalism Suspect in NYC
       Worked for Obama Campaign in 2008, Reports Say," *Fox News*,
       November 4, 2018, accessed December 12, 2018, *https://www.*
       foxnews.com/us/synagogue-vandalism-suspect-in-nyc-worked-
       for-obama-campaign-in-2008-reports-say.

138   Breanna Edwards, "'We Don't Tip Terrorist': Customer Banned
       from Texas Restaurant after Leaving Server Racist Note," *The*
       Root, July 19, 2018, accessed December 12, 2018, *https://www.*
       theroot.com/we-dont-tip-terrorist-customer-banned-from-tex-
       as-resta-1827712109?utm_source=theroot_twitter&utm_medi-
       um=socialflow.

139   Clarke Finney, "'We Don't Tip Terrorist,'" Your Basin, July 16,
       2018, accessed December 12, 2018, *https://www.yourbasin.com/*
       news/-we-don-t-tip-terrorist-/1306270175.

140   Eli Rosenberg and Kristine Phillips, "Waiter Faked Story That
       Customer Wrote 'We Don't Tip Terrorist' on Receipt, Restaurant
       Says," *The Washington Post*, July 23, 2018, accessed December
       12, 2018, *https://www.washingtonpost.com/news/post-nation/*
       wp/2018/07/23/waiter-faked-story-that-customer-wrote-we-
       dont-tip-terrorist-on-receipt-restaurant-says/?utm_term=.
       bf7e54092f6d.

141   Emily Ferguson, "College Student Confuses Covered Lab
       Equipment With KKK Rally," *The Washington Free Beacon*,
       January 24, 2017, accessed December 12, 2018, *https://*
       freebeacon.com/issues/college-student-confuses-covered-lab-
       equipment-with-klan-rally/.

142   David Hernandez and Gary Warth, "Muslim Student Robbed at SDSU in Apparent Hate Crime," *The San Diego Union-Tribune*, November 10, 2016, accessed December 12, 2018, *https://www. sandiegouniontribune.com/news/public-safety/sd-me-sdsu-robbery-20161110-story.html*.

143   R. Stickney, "SDSU Police: No Suspect in Attack on Muslim Student," *NBC 7 San Diego*, January 10, 2017, accessed December 12, 2018, *https://www.nbcsandiego. com/news/local/SDSU-Police-Attack-on-Muslim-Student-Unfounded-410296485.html*.

144   Jennifer Kabbany, "'Report Illegal Aliens; America Is a White Nation' Posters Hung – by Liberal Student Diversity Group," *The College Fix*, March 23, 2017, accessed December 12, 2018, *https://www.thecollegefix.com/report-illegal-aliens-america-white-nation-posters-hung-liberal-student-diversity-group/*.

145   "College Diversity Org Apologizes After 'White Nation' Poster Experiment," *WCCO CBS Minnesota*, March 21, 2017, accessed December 12, 2018, *https://minnesota.cbslocal.com/2017/03/21/gustavus-diversity-experiment/*.

146   Nathan Rubbelke, "CONFIRMED: Racist Note That Prompted St. Olaf College Shut down Is Hate-crime Hoax," *The College Fix*, May 10, 2017, accessed December 12, 2018, *https://www.thecollegefix.com/confirmed-racist-note-prompted-st-olaf-college-shut-hate-crime-hoax/*.

147   Lindsey Bever, "Protests Erupt, Classes Canceled after Racist Notes Enrage a Minnesota College," *The Washington Post*, May 1, 2017, accessed December 12, 2018, *https://www.washingtonpost.com/news/grade-point/wp/2017/05/01/protests-erupt-classes-canceled-after-rac-*

*ist-notes-enrage-a-minnesota-college/?noredirect=on&utm_*
term=.034a0de53381.

148 "Black Student Leaving K-State over Racist Graffiti on Car,"
Business Insider, November 1, 2017, accessed December 12,
2018, *https://www.businessinsider.com/ap-black-student-leav-*
ing-k-state-over-racist-graffiti-on-car-2017-11.

149 Willis Scott, "Police Say K-State Noose May Not Be Racist Act,"
KSNT, November 13, 2017, accessed December 12, 2018, *https://*
www.ksnt.com/news/local-news/police-say-k-state-noose-may-
not-be-racist_20180306032511331/1011470061.

150 "ISU Professor Arrested, Accused of Making up Threats and
Attack," *Tribune Star*, April 21, 2017, accessed December
12, 2018, *https://www.tribstar.com/news/isu-professor-*
arrested-accused-of-making-up-threats-and-attack/
article_c7ca5b60-26d9-11e7-a35a-0f3c7868f652.html.

151 Kelly Maricle, "Woman Charged with Arson in Fire at Des
Moines Mosque," *13 WHO TV*, June 23, 2017, accessed
December 12, 2018, *https://whotv.com/2017/06/23/*
woman-arrested-for-arson-in-fire-at-des-moines-mosque/.

152 Nancy Coleman, "On Average, 9 Mosques Have Been Targeted
Every Month This Year," CNN, August 7, 2017, accessed
December 12, 2018, *https://www.cnn.com/2017/03/20/us/*
mosques-targeted-2017-trnd/index.html.

153 "Anti-Defamation League Backs Lesbian Couple in Parker
Graffiti Case," *The Denver Post*, November 1, 2011, accessed
February 5, 2019, *https://www.denverpost.com/2011/11/01/*
anti-defamation-league-backs-lesbian-couple-in-parker-graffi-
ti-case/.

154   Joey Bunch, "Parker Lesbian Couple Charged with Staging Anti-Gay Offense to Accuse HOA after Spat over Dogs," *The Denver Post*, May 17, 2012, accessed February 5, 2019, *https://www.denverpost.com/2012/05/17/parker-lesbian-couple-charged-with-staging-anti-gay-offense-to-accuse-hoa-after-spat-over-dogs-2/*.

155   Travis Gettys, "Baltimore Woman's 'Relentlessly Gay' Fundraiser Revealed as Apparent Hoax," *Raw Story*, July 2, 2015, accessed December 12, 2018, *https://www.rawstory.com/2015/07/baltimore-womans-relentlessly-gay-fundraiser-revealed-as-apparent-hoax/*.

156   Claire Hodgson, "Woman Who Was Told Her Garden Is 'relentlessly Gay' Responds in the BEST Way," *Cosmopolitan*, June 19, 2015, accessed December 12, 2018, *https://www.cosmopolitan.com/uk/reports/news/a36594/woman-relentlessly-gay-garden/*.

157   "CNN Hosts Display Own Controversial 'Hands Up,'" Sally Kohn on CNN, December 14, 2014, accessed December 12, 2018, video, 00:43, *https://www.youtube.com/watch?v=ha1ljAbOPnY*.

158   Leah Barkoukis, "'Hands Up, Don't Shoot' Ranked One of 2015's Biggest Lies," *Townhall*, December 14, 2015, accessed December 12, 2018, *https://townhall.com/tipsheet/leahbarkoukis/2015/12/14/hands-up-dont-shoot-ranked-one-of-biggest-lies-of-year-n2093627*.

159   Emma Green, "A Black Church Burned in the Name of Trump," *The Atlantic*, November 2, 2016, accessed December 12, 2018, *https://www.theatlantic.com/politics/archive/2016/11/a-black-church-burned-in-the-name-of-trump/506246/*.

160   Corky Siemaszko, "Mississippi Church Torched and Vandalized with Pro-Trump Slogan," *NBC News*, November 2, 2016,

accessed December 12, 2018, *https://www.nbcnews.com/ storyline/2016-election-day/mississippi-church-torched-vandalized-pro-trump-slogan-n676816.*

161   Hillary Clinton (@HillaryClinton), "The perpetrators who set the Hopewell M.B. Church…" Twitter Tweet, November 16, 2016, accessed December 12, 2018, *http://archive.is/LgMbU.*

162   "Clinton Stirs Anger by Claiming She Carries Hot Sauce in Her Bag, like Beyoncé," *The Week*, April 18, 2016, accessed December 12, 2018, *https://theweek.com/speedreads/619127/clinton-stirs-anger-by-claiming-carries-hot-sauce-bag-like-beyonc.*

163   Kenya Downs, "Assailants Set Fire to Black Mississippi Church, Spray Paint 'Vote Trump,'" *PBS*, November 2, 2016, accessed December 12, 2018, *https://www.pbs.org/newshour/nation/ decades-burning-black-churches-tool-voter-suppression.*

164   Agence France-Presse, "Black Church Defaced by Trump Graffiti Was Destroyed by Arson, Say Officials," *The Telegraph*, November 3, 2016, accessed December 12, 2018, *https://www. telegraph.co.uk/news/2016/11/03/black-church-defaced-by-trump-graffiti-was-destroyed-by-arson-sa/.*

165   Justin Glawe, "A Burned Down Black Church Shows President Trump Wouldn't Condemn His Own Terrorists," *The Daily Beast*, November 6, 2016, accessed December 12, 2018, *https:// www.thedailybeast.com/a-burned-down-black-church-shows-president-trump-wouldnt-condemn-his-own-terrorists.*

166   Luke Rohlfing, "VIDEO: Antifa Threatens Tucker Carlson At His Home 'We Know Where You Sleep At Night,'" *Big League Politics*, November 7, 2018, accessed December 12, 2018, *https://bigleaguepolitics.com/*

video-antifa-threatens-tucker-carlson-at-his-home-we-know-where-you-sleep-at-night/.

167 Guy Benson, "Chilling Details: Tucker Carlson's Terrified Wife Hid in the Pantry As Antifa Thugs Damaged Her Home," *Townhall*, November 8, 2018, accessed December 12, 2018, *https://townhall.com/tipsheet/guybenson/2018/11/08/chilling-new-details-of-the-menacing-protest-at-tucker-carlsons-home-n2535567.*

168 John Philip Jenkins, "Terrorism," *Encyclopædia Britannica*, accessed December 12, 2018, *https://www.britannica.com/topic/terrorism.*

169 John Nolte, "No Empathy: Vox's Matt Yglesias Defends 'Terrorizing' Tucker Carlson's 'Family,'" *Breitbart*, November 8, 2018, accessed December 12, 2018, *https://www.breitbart.com/politics/2018/11/08/vox-matt-yglesias-defends-terrorizing-tucker-carlsons-family/.*

170 Soledad O'Brien (@soledadobrien), "Yes well when you're a racist, saying..." Twitter Tweet, November 10, 2018, accessed December 12, 2018, *http://archive.is/Gnp3X.*

171 Peter D'Abrosca, "WATCH: CNN's Cuomo Stands with Violent Antifa Members: 'All Punches Not Equal Morally,'" *Big League Politics*, August 14, 2018, accessed December 12, 2018, *https://bigleaguepolitics.com/watch-cnns-cuomo-stands-with-violent-antifa-members-all-punches-not-equal-morally/.*

172 Ian Schwartz, "Don Lemon Defends Antifa: 'No Organization Is Perfect,'" *RealClear Politics*, August 28, 2018, accessed December 12, 2018, *https://www.realclearpolitics.com/*

video/2018/08/28/don_lemon_defends_antifa_no_organiza-
tion_is_perfect.html

173 Justin Caruso, "CNN's Don Lemon Defends Antifa Harassment of Ted Cruz: 'That's What He Signed Up For,'" *Breitbart*,
September 26, 2018, accessed December 12, 2018, *https://www.
breitbart.com/the-media/2018/09/26/cnns-don-lemon-defends-
antifa-harassment-of-ted-cruz-thats-what-he-signed-up-for/*.

174 "Smash Racism DC," Facebook page, accessed December 12,
2018, *http://archive.is/J8OLV*.

175 Victor Morton, "Don Lemon Defends Protesters Who Harassed
Ted Cruz, Wife at Restaurant: 'It Goes with the Territory,'" *The
Washington Times*, September 26, 2018, accessed December
12, 2018, *https://www.washingtontimes.com/news/2018/sep/26/
don-lemon-defends-protesters-who-harassed-ted-cruz/*.

176 Chris Pleasance and Charlotte Dean, "DC Restaurant Hires
Security and Owner Pleads for Customers to Return as it
Recovers From 'PR Disaster' After Mob of Anti-Kavanaugh
Protesters Confronted Ted Cruz and His Wife Over
Dinner," *Daily Mail*, October 2, 2018, accessed December
12, 2018, *https://www.dailymail.co.uk/news/article-6230311/
DC-restaurant-hires-security-Ted-Cruz-confronted-Kavanaugh-
protesters.html*.

177 Peter D'Abrosca, "Loser Who Assaulted Teens and Stole
MAGA Hat Is 30-Year-Old Cosplayer With Long Rap Sheet,"
Big League Politics, July 05, 2018, accessed December 12, 2018,
*https://bigleaguepolitics.com/loser-who-assaulted-teens-and-
stole-maga-hat-is-30-year-old-cosplayer-with-long-rap-sheet/*.

178   Marc Lamont Hill (@marclamonthill), "I actually don't advo-
       cate throwing drinks..." Twitter Tweet, July 5, 2018, accessed
       December 12, 2018, *http://archive.is/GY4gK*.

179   Peter D'Abrosca, "CNN's Marc Lamont Hill Agrees With
       Hamas, Calls for Total Destruction of Israel," *Big League Poli-
       tics*, November 28, 2018, accessed December 12, 2018, *https://
       bigleaguepolitics.com/cnns-marc-lamont-hill-agrees-with-
       hamas-calls-for-total-destruction-of-israel/*.

180   Donie O'Sullivan, Drew Griffin, and Scott Bronstein,
       "The Unwitting: The Trump Supporters Used by Russia,"
       CNN Business, February 20, 2018, accessed December
       12, 2018, *https://money.cnn.com/2018/02/20/media/inter-
       net-research-agency-unwitting-trump-supporters/index.
       html?sr=twCNN022018internet-research-agency-unwit-
       ting-trump-supporters0903PMStory*.

181   CNN (@CNN), "A Florida woman who ran a Trump supporters
       page that..." Twitter Tweet, February 20, 2018, accessed
       December 12, 2018, *http://archive.is/BBvWy*.

182   Charlie Nash, "Woman Receives Abuse, Violent Threats After
       CNN Tracks Down, Publicly Shames Her for Sharing 'Russian'
       Event on Facebook," *Breitbart*, February 21, 2018, accessed
       December 12, 2018, *https://www.breitbart.com/tech/2018/02/21/
       woman-receives-abuse-violent-threats-after-cnn-tracks-down-
       publicly-shames-her-for-sharing-russian-event-on-facebook/*.

183   Andrew Kaczynski, "How CNN Found the Reddit User behind
       the Trump Wrestling GIF," CNN, July 5, 2017, accessed
       December 12, 2018, *https://www.cnn.com/2017/07/04/politics/
       kfile-reddit-user-trump-tweet/index.html*.

184   Joe Concha, "CNN Host Bourdain Jokes about
       Poisoning Trump," *The Hill*, September 15, 2017, accessed

December 12, 2018, *https://thehill.com/homenews/ media/350857-cnn-host-bourdain-jokes-about-poisoning-trump.*

185 "Who Is 'designated Survivor' at Inauguration?" CNN, January 18, 2017, accessed December 12, 2018, video, 3:28, *https://www. youtube.com/watch?time_continue=68&v=qxIG4dduqy0.*

186 "Thomas A. Shannon, Jr.," Arnold & Porter, accessed December 12, 2018, *https://www.arnoldporter.com/en/people/s/ shannon-thomas.*

187 Martin Savidge and Dana Ford, "'Trump Is a Bully,' Says Man Who Rushed Stage," CNN, March 14, 2016, accessed December 12, 2018, *https://www.cnn.com/2016/03/13/politics/thomas- dimassimo-donald-trump-protester-interview/index.html.*

188 Ben Kew, "MSNBC 'Counter-Terrorism Analyst' Calls for ISIS Bombing of Trump Property," *Breitbart*, April 19, 2017, accessed December 12, 2018, *https://www.breitbart.com/ the-media/2017/04/19/msnbc-counter-terrorism-analyst-calls- for-isis-bombing-of-trump-property/.*

189 Ryan Saavedra, "WATCH: Joy Reid Launches Vile Attack On Conservatives, Panel Hopes They 'Die Off'," *The Daily Wire*, March 7, 2018, accessed December 12, 2018, *https://www. dailywire.com/news/27956/bigot-joy-reid-launches-vile-attack- conservatives-ryan-saavedra.*

190 Benjy Sarlin, "Antifa Violence Is Ethical? This Author Explains Why," *NBC News*, August 26, 2017, accessed December 12, 2018, *https://www.nbcnews.com/politics/white-house/ antifa-violence-ethical-author-explains-why-n796106.*

191 "Five Novelists Imagine Trump's Next Chapter," *The New York Times*, October 23, 2018, accessed December 12, 2018, *https:// www.nytimes.com/2018/10/23/books/review/trumps-next-chapter.html.*

192 "Democrats: Do Not Surrender the Judiciary," *The New York Times*, July 6, 2018, accessed December 12, 2018, *https://www.nytimes.com/2018/07/06/opinion/ democrats-fight-trump-supreme-court.html?action=click&pg-type=Homepage&clickSource=story-heading&module=opin-ion-c-col-left-region&gion=opinion-c-col-left-region&WT. nav=opinion-c-col-left-region.*

193 "The Godfather," Fandom Wiki, accessed December 12, 2018, *http://listofdeaths.wikia.com/wiki/The_Godfather.*

194 John Bowden, "Rosie O'Donnell on Trump Sending Military to Border: I Want to Send Them to the White House," *The Hill*, October 18, 2018, accessed December 12, 2018, *https://thehill. com/blogs/in-the-know/in-the-know/412166-rosie-odonnell-on-trump-sending-military-to-border-i-want-to.*

195 Brian Flood, "New Yorker Unveils Polarizing Cover Depicting Trump Falling down Escalator onto His Face," *Fox News*, July 19, 2018, accessed December 12, 2018, *https://www.foxnews. com/entertainment/new-yorker-unveils-polarizing-cover-de-picting-trump-falling-down-escalator-onto-his-face.*

196 Francoise Mouly, "Barry Blitt's 'Thumbs-Up,'" *The New Yorker*, July 19, 2018, accessed December 12, 2018, *https://www.newyorker.com/culture/cover-story/ cover-story-2018-07-30?mbid=social_twitter.*

197 Will Ricciardella, "HuffPo Pulls Article Calling
For 'Ultimate Punishment' Of Trump," *The
Daily Caller*, June 14, 2017, accessed December
12, 2018, *https://dailycaller.com/2017/06/14/
huffpo-pulls-article-calling-for-ultimate-punishment-of-trump/*.

198 Peter D'Abrosca, "FAKE NEWS: Here Are the Press Outlets
Who Wrongly Said Sarah Huckabee Sanders Shared 'Manipulated' Acosta Video," *Big League Politics*, November 9, 2018,
accessed December 12, 2018, *https://bigleaguepolitics.com/
fake-news-here-are-the-press-outlets-who-wrongly-said-sarah-
huckabee-sanders-shared-manipulated-acosta-video/*.

199 Bethania Palma, "White House Press Secretary Blasted for
Sharing Infowars Video to Bar Reporter," *Snopes*, November
8, 2018, accessed December 12, 2018, *https://www.snopes.com/
news/2018/11/08/white-house-press-secretary-blasted-for-shar-
ing-infowars-video-to-attack-reporter/*.

200 Jon Levine, "Kellyanne Conway Admits White House's
'Karate Chop' Video of Jim Acosta Was 'Sped Up,'" *The Wrap*,
November 12, 2018, accessed December 12, 2018, *https://www.
thewrap.com/kellyanne-conway-admits-white-houses-karate-
chop-video-of-jim-acosta-was-sped-up/*.

201 "Disclosures, Things to know about how we operate," Snopes,
accessed December 12, 2018, *https://www.snopes.com/
disclosures/*.

202 "Did President Trump Cancel Protections for Whales and Sea
Turtles?" *Snopes*, accessed December 12, 2018, *https://www.
snopes.com/fact-check/trump-whales-sea-turtles/*.

203   Peter D'Abrosca, "BLP Catches Snopes in Another
      Misleading 'Fact Check,'" *Big League Politics*, July 13, 2018,
      accessed December 12, 2018, *https://bigleaguepolitics.com/
      blp-catches-snopes-in-another-misleading-fact-check/*.

204   Eric Swalwell (@RepSwalwell), "And it would be a short war my
      friend..." Twitter Tweet, November 16, 2018, accessed December
      12, 2018, *http://archive.is/gYPnl*.

205   Eric Swalwell (@RepSwalwell), "Well this should end the
      faux-outrage..." Twitter Tweet, November 19, 2018, accessed
      December 12, 2018, *http://archive.is/eTvlX*.

206   "Did Democrats Elect Four Horrible People?" *Snopes*, accessed
      December 12, 2018, *https://www.snopes.com/fact-check/
      democrats-elected-four-people/*.

207   Ilhan Omar (@IlhanMN), "Israel has hypnotized the world, may
      Allah awaken..." Twitter Tweet, November 16, 2012, accessed
      December 12, 2018, *http://archive.is/hR31K*.

208   Bill McCarthy, "Corey Stewart's History With the Far
      Right, Explained," *PolitiFact*, June 20, 2018, accessed
      December 12, 2018, *https://www.politifact.com/
      truth-o-meter/statements/2018/jun/20/corey-stewart/
      corey-stewarts-history-far-right-explained/*.

209   "Did 'Melbourne Antifa' Claim Responsibility for the Vegas
      Massacre?" *Snopes*, accessed December 12, 2018, *https://www.
      snopes.com/fact-check/did-melbourne-antifa-claim-responsi-
      bility-for-the-vegas-massacre/*.

210   Peter D'Abrosca, "FACT CHECK: Did Snopes Source
      an Anonymous Blogger to Challenge the Veracity of an

Established News Source?" *Big League Politics*, May 17, 2018, accessed December 12, 2018, *https://bigleaguepolitics.com/ fact-check-did-snopes-source-an-anonymous-blogger-to-chal- lenge-the-veracity-of-an-established-news-source/*.

211 "Planned Parenthood Defends Bill Cosby: 'Sexual Assault Is Only 3% Of What He Does,'" *The Babylon Bee*, April 27, 2018, accessed December 12, 2018, *https://babylonbee.com/news/ planned-parenthood-defends-bill-cosby-sexual-assault-is-only- 3-of-what-he-does/*.

212 "Did Planned Parenthood Defend Bill Cosby?" *Snopes*, accessed December 12, 2018, *https://www.snopes.com/ fact-check/did-planned-parenthood-defend-bill-cosby/*.

213 "Joel Osteen Sails Luxury Yacht Through Flooded Houston to Pass out Copies of His Book?" *Snopes*, accessed December 12, 2018, *https://www.snopes.com/fact-check/ osteen-yacht-houston-book-hurricane/*.

214 "Is Playing Christmas Music Before Thanksgiving Now a Federal Crime?" *Snopes*, accessed December 12, 2018, *https://www.snopes.com/fact-check/ playing-christmas-music-federal-crime/*.

215 "Did ICE Hurl a Pregnant Woman Over a Border Wall?" *Snopes*, accessed February 17, 2019, *https://www.snopes.com/ fact-check/ice-hurl-pregnant-woman-border-wall/*.

216 "Did a Judge Order That a White Woman Be Tried As an African-American?" *Snopes*, accessed December 12, 2018, *https://www.snopes.com/fact-check/ judge-white-woman-tried-african-american/*.

217 "Shelling from Royal Caribbean's M.S. 'Allure' Sinks Carnival Cruise Vessel That Crossed into Disputed Waters?" *Snopes*,

accessed December 12, 2018, *https://www.snopes.com/ fact-check/royal-caribbeans-sinks-carnival-cruise/*.

218 "Hundreds of Cuban Refugees Clinging to Air Force One on Flight Back to U.S." *Snopes*, accessed December 12, 2018, *https://www.snopes.com/fact-check/ cuban-refugees-clinging-to-air-force-one/*.

219 "Did Ohio Replace Lethal Injection with a Head-Ripping-Off Machine?" *Snopes*, accessed December 12, 2018, *https://www. snopes.com/fact-check/head-shot/*.

220 Aaron Sharockman, "PolitiFact Gains Nonprofit Status with Move to the Poynter Institute," *PolitiFact*, February 12, 2018, accessed December 12, 2018, *https://www. politifact.com/truth-o-meter/article/2018/feb/12/ politifact-gains-nonprofit-status-move-poynter-ins/*.

221 Barbara Joanna Lucas, "DISHONEST FACT-CHECKERS: How Fact-checkers Trivialize Lies by Politicians and Under- mine Truth-seeking," *Capital Research Center*, March 10, 2017, accessed December 12, 2018, *https://capitalresearch.org/ article/dishonest-fact-checkers/*.

222 "Our Supporters 2016," Center for American Progress, accessed December 12, 2018, *https://www.americanprogress.org/ our-supporters-2016/*.

223 David Martosko, "Left-Wing Foundations Lavish Millions On Media Matters," *The Daily Caller*, February 17, 2012, accessed December 12, 2018, *https://dailycaller.com/2012/02/17/ left-wing-foundations-lavish-millions-on-media-matters/*.

224 Sherrie St James, "FLORIDA POLLS VOTE RIGGED?!!! READ FIRST NOT..." Facebook post, November 6, 2018, accessed December 12, 2018, *http://archive.is/d7ifR.*

225 Ciara O'Rourke, "No, MSNBC Didn't Call the Florida Governor's for Andrew Gillum before Election," *PolitiFact*, November 6, 2018, accessed December 12, 2018, *https://www.politifact.com/facebook-fact-checks/statements/2018/nov/06/blog-posting/no-msnbc-didnt-call-florida-governors-andrew-gillu/.*

226 Miriam Valverde, "Facebook Meme Makes False Claims About Benefits to Immigrants Who Cross Border Illegally," *PolitiFact*, November 8, 2018, accessed December 12, 2018, *https://www.politifact.com/facebook-fact-checks/statements/2018/nov/08/viral-image/facebook-meme-misleads-about-benefits-immigrants-w/.*

227 Manu Raju and Jeremy Herb, "Email Pointed Trump Campaign to WikiLeaks Documents," CNN, December 08, 2017, accessed December 12, 2018, *https://www.cnn.com/2017/12/08/politics/email-effort-give-trump-campaign-wikileaks-documents/index.html.*

228 Oliver. Darcy, "CNN Corrects Story on Email to Trumps about Wikileaks," CNN *Business*, December 8, 2018, accessed December 12, 2018, *https://money.cnn.com/2017/12/08/media/cnn-correction-email-story/index.html.*

229 Kaitlyn Schallhorn, "Obama-era Russian Uranium One Deal: What to Know," *Fox News*, February 8, 2018, accessed December 12, 2018, *https://www.foxnews.com/politics/obama-era-russian-uranium-one-deal-what-to-know.*

230 Gloria Borger et al., "Comey Unlikely to Judge on Obstruction," CNN, June 7, 2017, accessed December 12, 2018, *https://www.cnn.com/2017/06/06/politics/ comey-testimony-refute-trump-russian-investigation/*.

231 Philip Ewing, "Cohen's Account Of Russia Talks Raises Questions About Trump Jr. 2017 Testimony," *NPR*, November 30, 2017, accessed December 12, 2018, *http://archive.is/Wh3mF*.

232 Brian Ross, Matthew Mosk, and Josh Margolin, "Flynn Prepared to Testify That Trump Directed Him to Contact Russians about ISIS, Confidant Says," *ABC News*, December 01, 2017, accessed December 12, 2018, *https://abcnews.go.com/Politics/michael-flynn-charged-making-false-statements-fbi-documents/ story?id=50849354*.

233 Erik Wemple, "Why Suspend ABC News's Brian Ross over Michael Flynn Mistake?" *The Washington Post*, December 04, 2017, accessed December 12, 2018, *https://www.wash-ingtonpost.com/blogs/erik-wemple/wp/2017/12/04/ why-suspend-abc-newss-brian-ross-over-michael-flynn-mis-take/?noredirect=on&utm_term=.50bc52f3bc99*.

234 Josh Rogin, "The State Department's Entire Senior Administrative Team Just Resigned," *The Washington Post*, January 26, 2017, accessed December 12, 2018, *https://www. washingtonpost.com/news/josh-rogin/wp/2017/01/26/ the-state-departments-entire-senior-management-team-just-re-signed/?noredirect=on&utm_term=.2ae8b027c4e0*.

235 Sheera Frenkel (@sheeraf), "Asked a US diplomat friend how he felt about..." Twitter Tweet, January 26, 2017, accessed December 12, 2018, *http://archive.is/50pSC*.

236 Becket Adams, "Media's Trump Hysteria Is Doing More Harm than Good," *Washington Examiner*, January 27, 2017, accessed December 12, 2018, *https://www.washingtonexaminer.com/ medias-trump-hysteria-is-doing-more-harm-than-good.*

237 Josh Susong, "FBI Releases New Photos, Video of 2011 Giffords Shooting," *azcentral*, April 5, 2018, accessed December 12, 2018, *https://www.azcentral.com/story/news/local/ arizona/2018/04/05/fbi-releases-new-photos-video-2011-gabby-giffords-shooting/489367002/.*

238 "America's Lethal Politics," *The New York Times*, June 14, 2017, accessed December 12, 2018, *https://www.nytimes. com/2017/06/14/opinion/steve-scalise-congress-shot-alexan-dria-virginia.html.*

239 Peter D'Abrosca, "Rabid Anti-Trump Leftist Attempts to Stab GOP Congressional Candidate," *Big League Politics*, September 11, 2018, accessed December 12, 2018, *https:// bigleaguepolitics.com/rabid-anti-trump-leftist-attempts-to-stab-gop-congressional-candidate/.*

240 Eli Rosenberg, "Stephen Miller Used to Eat Glue, His Third-grade Teacher Said. The School Placed Her on Leave," *The Washington Post*, October 12, 2018, accessed December 12, 2018, *https://www.washingtonpost.com/politics/2018/10/12/ stephen-miller-used-eat-glue-his-third-grade-teacher-said-school-placed-her-leave/.*

241 Kate Sullivan, "Ivanka Trump Used Personal Account for Emails about Government Business," CNN, November 20, 2018, accessed December 12, 2018, *https://www.cnn.com/2018/11/19/ politics/ivanka-trump-personal-email-account/index.html.*

242   Brooke Singman, "Newly Released Clinton Emails Include
       Classified Messages, Show Knowledge of Security Prob-
       lems: Watchdog," *Fox News*, January 19, 2018, accessed
       December 12, 2018, *https://www.foxnews.com/politics/
       newly-released-clinton-emails-include-classified-messag-
       es-show-knowledge-of-security-problems-watchdog*.

243   Martin Longman, "The Hunt for Clinton's 33,000
       Deleted Emails," *Washington Monthly*, January 2, 2018,
       accessed December 12, 2018, *https://washingtonmonthly.
       com/2018/01/02/the-hunt-for-clintons-33000-deleted-emails/*.

244   Sarah Westwood, "Clinton's Use of BleachBit Avoided
       'Money Trail' in Email Destruction," *Washington Examiner*,
       August 29, 2016, accessed December 12, 2018, *https://www.
       washingtonexaminer.com/clintons-use-of-bleachbit-avoided-
       money-trail-in-email-destruction*.

245   Brian Krassenstein (@krassenstein),"Dear Donald, Where are
       the "Lock her up..." November 19, 2018, accessed December 12,
       2018, *http://archive.is/671KK*.

246   Joe DePaolo, "CNN's Jeffrey Toobin Tears Into Ivanka For
       Using a Private Email Account: 'Incredible Arrogance' With
       a 'Measure of Stupidity,'" *MEDIAite*, November 19, 2018,
       accessed December 12, 2018, *https://www.mediaite.com/online/
       cnns-jeffrey-toobin-tears-into-ivanka-for-using-a-private-email-
       account-incredible-arrogance-with-a-little-measure-
       of-stupidity/*.

247   Nicholas Kulish et al., "Trump's Immigration Policies
       Explained," *The New York Times*, February 21, 2017, accessed
       December 12, 2018, *https://www.nytimes.com/2017/02/21/us/
       trump-immigration-policies-deportation.html*.

248 Jennifer Medina and Julia Preston, "U.S. Immigration Laws Face New Scrutiny After Killings," *The New
York Times*, October 28, 2014, accessed December 12,
2018, *https://www.nytimes.com/2014/10/29/us/mexi-
can-held-in-shootings-was-deported-after-arrests.
html?action=click&contentCollection=U.S.&module=RelatedCov-
erage&ion=EndOfArticle&pgtype=article.*

249 "US Mid-terms Latest: Trump's Immigration Ad Draws Criticism," *BBC News*, November 1, 2018, accessed December 12,
2018, *https://www.bbc.com/news/world-us-canada-46055215.*

250 Brian Stelter and Oliver Darcy, "NBC and Fox Finally Stop
Running Trump's Racist Ad after It Was Viewed by Millions,"
CNN, November 5, 2018, accessed December 12, 2018, *https://
www.cnn.com/2018/11/05/media/nbc-trump-immigration-ad/
index.html.*

251 "Networks, Facebook Drop Trump's Anti-immigrant Ad," *Al
Jazeera*, November 5, 2018, accessed December 12, 2018,
*https://www.aljazeera.com/news/2018/11/networks-facebook-
drop-trump-anti-immigrant-ad-181105213321742.html.*

252 Zachary Basu, "NBC, Fox News, Facebook Pull Controversial Trump Anti-immigration Ad," *Axios*, November 5,
2018, accessed December 12, 2018, *https://www.axios.com/
nbc-fox-news-pull-controversial-trump-immigration-ad-
d7f1798d-df0a-4dc4-b9f9-e11e46382d69.html.*

253 Soo Rin Kim and Katherine Faulders, "How Trump's Controversial Anti-immigrant Video Skirts Rules for Political
Ads," *ABC News*, November 2, 2018, accessed December
12, 2018, *https://abcnews.go.com/Politics/trumps-con-
troversial-anti-immigrant-video-skirts-rules-political/
story?id=58912789.*

254   Steven A. Camarota, "Americans Prefer Illegal Immigrants
      Head Home," *Center for Immigration Studies*, February
      6, 2013, accessed December 12, 2018, *https://cis.org/
      Americans-Prefer-Illegal-Immigrants-Head-Home*.

255   Philip Bump, "Trump Points at the Media: You're to Blame for
      Encouraging Violence," *The Washington Post*, November 2,
      2018, accessed February 7, 2019, *www.washingtonpost.com/
      politics/2018/11/02/trump-points-media-youre-blame-encour-
      aging-violence/?noredirect=on*.

256   Kristen Gillibrand, "Tamika Mallory, Bob Bland, Carmen
      Perez and Linda Sarsour," *Time*, 2017, accessed December
      12, 2018, *http://time.com/collection/2017-time-100/4742711/
      tamika-mallory-bob-bland-carmen-perez-linda-sarsour/*.

257   Richard Wheatstone, "Woman Faces Being Stoned to
      Death for Adultery - While Male Partner to Receive 100
      Lashes," *Mirror*, November 27, 2015, accessed December
      12, 2018, *https://www.mirror.co.uk/news/world-news/
      woman-stoned-death-adultery-saudi-6912835*.

258   Shannon Van Sant, "Saudi Arabia Lifts Ban On Female
      Drivers," *NPR*, June 24, 2018, accessed December 12,
      2018, *https://www.npr.org/2018/06/24/622990978/
      saudi-arabia-lifts-ban-on-women-drivers*.

259   Agence France-Presse, "Saudi Arabia Criticised
      for 48 Beheadings in Four Months of 2018," *The
      Guardian*, April 26, 2018, accessed December 12, 2018,
      *https://www.theguardian.com/world/2018/apr/26/
      saudi-arabia-criticised-over-executions-for-drug-offences*.

260   Laura Loomer, "Linda Sarsour, Muslim Candidates Tied To
      Father Of Jihadi Who Trained Children To Become 'School
      Shooters' In New Mexico," *Big League Politics*, August 9, 2018,

accessed December 12, 2018, *https://bigleaguepolitics.com/
linda-sarsour-muslim-candidates-tied-to-father-of-jihadi-who-
trained-children-to-become-school-shooters-in-new-mexico/*.

261   Ben Sales, "Linda Sarsour Apologizes to Woman's
      March Jewish Members for Slow Response to
      Anti-Semitism," *Haaretz*, November 21, 2018, accessed
      December 12, 2018, *https://www.haaretz.com/us-news/
      linda-sarsour-apologizes-to-woman-s-march-members-for-slow-
      response-to-anti-semitism-1.6675453*.

262   "Video of Louis Farrakhan Comparing Jews to
      Termites Removed from Facebook," *Jewish Tele-
      graphic Agency*, October 21, 2018, accessed December
      12, 2018, *https://www.jta.org/2018/10/21/news-opinion/
      farrakhan-termites-video-removed-facebook*.

263   Joel B. Pollak, "Democrat Rashida Tlaib Dances with Pales-
      tinian Flag at Victory Party," *Breitbart*, November 7, 2018,
      accessed December 12, 2018, *https://www.breitbart.com/
      politics/2018/11/07/democrat-rashida-tlaib-dances-with-pales-
      tinian-flag-at-victory-party/*.

264   "Two Authorities, One Way, Zero Dissent," *Human
      Rights Watch*, October 23, 2018, accessed December
      12, 2018, *https://www.hrw.org/report/2018/10/23/
      two-authorities-one-way-zero-dissent/
      arbitrary-arrest-and-torture-under#page*.

265   Erin Cunningham, "Women in Iran Are Pulling off
      Their Headscarves – and Hoping for a 'Turning Point,'"
      The Washington Post, March 08, 2018, accessed
      December 12, 2018, *https://www.washingtonpost*.

com/world/women-in-iran-are-pulling-off-their-head-scarves--and-hoping-for-a-turning-point/2018/03/08/bb238a96-217c-11e8-946c-9420060cb7bd_story.html.

266 Laura Loomer, "Minnesota Congressional Candidate Speaks At Pro-HAMAS Fundraiser," *Big League Politics*, September 24, 2018, accessed December 12, 2018, *https://bigleaguepolitics.com/minnesota-congressional-candidate-speaks-at-pro-hamas-fundraiser/*.

267 "Congresswoman Omar Shares Support for BDS," *The Jerusalem Post*, November 14, 2018, accessed December 12, 2018, *https://www.jpost.com//American-Politics/Freshman-congresswoman-Ilhan-Omar-flip-flops-shares-support-for-BDS-571917*.

268 AWR Hawkins, "Study: 97.8% of Mass Shootings Since 1950 Occurred in 'Gun-Free Zones,'" *Breitbart*, November 20, 2018, accessed December 12, 2018, *https://www.breitbart.com/politics/2018/11/20/study-97-8-percent-mass-shootings-since-1950-gun-free-zones/*.

269 Andrew Glass, "Clinton Signs Assault Weapons Ban, Sept. 13, 1994," *POLITICO*. September 13, 2018, accessed December 12, 2018, *https://www.politico.com/story/2018/09/13/clinton-signs-assault-weapons-ban-sept-13-1994-813552*.

270 Peter Dujardin, "'Assault' Rifles vs. Handguns: Which Are the Bigger Problem?" *Daily Press*, March 21, 2018, accessed December 12, 2018, *https://www.dailypress.com/news/crime/dp-nws-assault-rifles-handgun-violence-20180312-story.html*.

271 Koronowski, Ryan. "Romaine Lettuce Is Too Dangerous to Be in Stores, but Guns Are Still Available 24 Hours per Day." *ThinkProgress*, November 23, 2018, accessed December 13, 2018, *https://thinkprogress.org/romaine-lettuce-recall-guns-always-available-d271c1b12859/*.

272   Paul Farhi, "Fareed Zakaria Suspended by CNN, Time for
       Plagiarism," *The Washington Post*. August 10, 2012, accessed
       December 13, 2018, *https://www.washingtonpost.com/lifestyle/
       style/fareed-zakaria-suspended-by-cnn-time-for-plagia-
       rism/2012/08/10/f6315e96-e335-11e1-ae7f-d2a13e249eb2_story.
       html?utm_term=.e5ad61a92ce3.*

273   Jill Lepore, "Battleground America," *The New Yorker*, April 23,
       2012 issue, accessed December 13, 2018, *https://www.newyorker.
       com/magazine/2012/04/23/battleground-america.*

274   "Fareed Zakaria Cleared by Time, CNN in Plagiarism Investiga-
       tion," *The Huffington Post*, August 16, 2012, accessed January
       16, 2019, *https://www.huffingtonpost.com/2012/08/16/fareed-
       zakaria-time-columns-review_n_1792081.html.*

275   Richard Leiby, "Columnist Fareed Zakaria Faces New Accusa-
       tions of Plagiarism," *The Washington Post*, August 19, 2014,
       accessed December 13, 2018, *https://www.washingtonpost.
       com/lifestyle/style/columnist-fareed-zakaria-faces-new-ac-
       cusations-of-plagiarism/2014/08/19/52bff872-27ed-11e4-958c-
       268a320a60ce_story.html?utm_term=.4517acb35099.*

276   Ryan Cooper, "Three Major Publications Have Acknowl-
       edged Plagiarism by Fareed Zakaria. Does CNN Have
       No Shame?" *The Week*, November 18, 2014, accessed
       December 13, 2018, *https://theweek.com/articles/442125/
       three-major-publications-have-acknowledged-plagiarism-by-
       fareed-zakaria-does-cnn-have-no-shame.*

277   Megan McArdle, "There's Little We Can Do to Prevent
       Another Massacre," *The Daily Beast*, December 17, 2012,
       accessed December 13, 2018, *https://www.thedailybeast.com/
       theres-little-we-can-do-to-prevent-another-massacre.*

278 Alyssa Milano, "Alyssa Milano: A 3D Printed Gun Is Download-able Death," CNN, July 31, 2018, accessed December 13, 2018, *https://www.cnn.com/2018/07/30/opinions/3d-printed-guns-opinion-alyssa-milano/index.html*.

279 Maurie Backman, "What the Average American Has -- and Needs -- in Emergency Savings," *USA Today*, May 22, 2018, accessed December 13, 2018, *https://www.usatoday.com/story/money/personalfinance/budget-and-spending/2018/05/22/what-average-american-needs-in-emergency-savings/35175419/*.

280 Peter D'Abrosca, "Cody Wilson Defies Court Order, Begins Selling Firearm CAD Files for 3-D Printing," *Big League Politics*, August 28, 2018, accessed December 13, 2018, *https://bigleaguepolitics.com/cody-wilson-defies-court-order-begins-selling-firearm-cad-files-for-3-d-printing/*.

281 Alyssa Milano, "Alyssa Milano on Witnessing The Kava-naugh Hearings & Our Government's War On Women," *Refinery29*, October 22, 2018, accessed December 13, 2018, *https://www.refinery29.com/en-us/2018/10/214647/alyssa-milano-kavanaugh-supreme-court-abortion-laws-essay*.

282 Joseph Curl, "Alyssa Milano Screeches At President Trump In Profane Rant, Gets Schooled (Again)," *The Daily Wire*, November 26, 2018, accessed December 13, 2018, *https://www.dailywire.com/news/38691/alyssa-milano-screeches-president-trump-profane-joseph-curl*.

283 "Other Countries That Celebrate Thanksgiving," *VOA*, November 22, 2018, accessed December 13, 2018, *https://*

www.voanews.com/a/other-countries-that-celebrate-thanks-giving/4668154.html.

284   Nick Schager, "Rob Reiner: President Trump Is a Russian 'Asset' and 'We Are in Dire Trouble,'" *The Daily Beast*, July 20, 2018, accessed December 13, 2018, *https://www.thedailybeast.com/ rob-reiner-president-trump-is-a-russian-asset-and-we-are-in-dire-trouble.*

285   Douglas Ernst, "Rob Reiner: Trump First President 'Supported by Mainstream Media,'" *The Washington Times*, June 9, 2018, accessed December 13, 2018, *https://www.washingtontimes.com/news/2018/jun/9/ rob-reiner-claims-donald-trump-first-president-sup/.*

286   "Rob Reiner: Trump Is Single Most Unqualified U.S. President," *Variety*, accessed December 13, 2018, *https://variety.com/ video/rob-reiner-trump-mentally-unfit/.*

287   Emily Birnbaum, "Rihanna on US Border Patrol Firing Tear Gas at Migrants: 'Terrorism,'" *The Hill*, November 26, 2018, accessed December 13, 2018, *https://thehill.com/latino/418252-rihanna-on-us-border-patrol-firing-tear-gas-at-migrants-terrorism.*

288   Lizzie Dearden, "Paris Attack Latest: Isis Claims Responsibility for Multiple Stabbings in Opera District," *The Independent,* May 13, 2018, accessed December 13, 2018, *https://www.independent.co.uk/news/world/europe/ paris-attack-latest-isis-terror-stabbing-islamist-opera-district-knife-dead-victims-french-police-a8349011.html.*

289   "ISIS-linked Gunman Shot Dead by French Police after Taking Hostages, Killing Three," *Haaretz*, March 23, 2018, accessed December 13, 2018, *https://www.haaretz.com/world-news/*

europe/hostage-situation-in-southern-france-gunman-claims-
isis-allegiance-1.5937301.

290   Laura Smith-Spark, Saskya Vandoorne, and Ray Sanchez, "Paris
      Shooting Casts Shadow Over Final Day of French Election
      Campaign," CNN, April 23, 2017, accessed December 13, 2018,
      *https://edition.cnn.com/2017/04/21/europe/paris-police-
      shooting-champs-elysees/index.html.*

291   Jennifer Harper, "Unprecedented Hostility: Broadcast Coverage
      of President Trump Still 90% Negative, Says Study," *The
      Washington Times*, March 6, 2018, accessed December 13,
      2018, *https://www.washingtontimes.com/news/2018/mar/6/
      trump-coverage-still-90-negative-says-new-study/.*

292   Paul Farhi, "Kevin Williamson Loses Atlantic Job after Contro-
      versy over Abortion Rhetoric," *The Washington Post*, April 5,
      2018, accessed December 13, 2018, *https://www.washingtonpost.
      com/lifestyle/style/kevin-williamson-loses-atlantic-job-af-
      ter-controversy-over-abortion-rhetoric/2018/04/05/3ab-
      19c4a-3900-11e8-9c0a-85d477d9a226_story.
      html?noredirect=on&utm_term=.442abd7c4160.*

293   Tina Nguyen, "Donald Trump Trolls the Media, Turns
      Phony 'Birther' Press Conference Into Hotel Infomer-
      cial," *The Hive*, September 16, 2016, accessed December
      13, 2018, *https://www.vanityfair.com/news/2016/09/
      donald-trump-birther-obama-press-conference.*

294   Kathleen Elkins, "Most Young Americans Prefer Socialism
      to Capitalism, New Report Finds," *CNBC*, August 14, 2018,
      accessed December 13, 2018, *https://www.cnbc.com/2018/08/14/
      fewer-than-half-of-young-americans-are-positive-about-capi-
      talism.html.*

295 Peter D'Abrosca, "Notorious Drag Queen Admits to
     'Grooming' Children," *Big League Politics*, November 29, 2018,
     accessed December 13, 2018, *https://bigleaguepolitics.com/*
     notorious-drag-queen-admits-to-grooming-children/.

296 Peter D'Abrosca, "Exclusive: California Teacher Wins 'Teacher
     of the Year' After FIVE-YEAR-OLD 'Transitions' In Class," *Big*
     League Politics, April 8, 2018, accessed December 13, 2018,
     https://bigleaguepolitics.com/exclusive-california-teacher-
     wins-teacher-year-five-year-old-transitions-class/.

297 "Hateful Conduct Policy," Twitter, accessed December
     13, 2018, *https://help.twitter.com/en/rules-and-policies/*
     hateful-conduct-policy.

298 Sean McElwee, "The Power of 'Abolish ICE,'" *The New York*
     Times, August 4, 2018, accessed December 13, 2018, *https://*
     www.nytimes.com/2018/08/04/opinion/sunday/abolish-ice-
     ocasio-cortez-democrats.html.

299 Dan Merica, "Clinton: it's time to abolish the Electoral College,"
     CNN, September 14, 2017, accessed December 13, 2018,
     https://www.cnn.com/2017/09/13/politics/hillary-clinton-
     anderson-cooper-electoral-college-cnntv/index.html.

300 Stephen Gutowski, "Landlord Tells Harvard Grad
     Student to Move Out Over Legally Owned Guns," *The*
     Washington Free Beacon, November 30, 2018, accessed
     December 13, 2018, *https://freebeacon.com/issues/*
     landlord-tells-harvard-student-move-legally-owned-guns/.

301 "Jeff Zucker Net Worth," *Celebrity Net Worth*, accessed
     December 13, 2018, *https://www.celebritynetworth.com/*
     richest-businessmen/ceos/jeff-zucker-net-worth/.

302 "Jeff Zucker's House," Virtual Globetrotting, accessed December 13, 2018, *https://virtualglobetrotting.com/map/jeff-zuckers-house/view/google/*.

303 Joel Anderson, "Anderson Cooper Net Worth: His Fortune at Age 51," *Yahoo! Finance*, June 1, 2018, accessed December 13, 2018, *https://finance.yahoo.com/news/anderson-cooper-net-worth-fortune-090000740.html*.

304 "Don Lemon Salary, Net Worth | How Much is CNN's Gay Host Worth?" WIKI Networth, September 16, 2018, accessed December 13, 2018, *http://wikinetworth.com/celebrities/don-lemon-salary-net-worth.html*.

305 "Brian Stelter – Know Him Better!" *Salary and Net Worth*, accessed December 13, 2018, *https://salaryandnetworth.com/brian-stelter-know-him-better/*.

306 "Rachel Maddow Net Worth," *Celebrity Net Worth*, accessed December 13, 2018, *https://www.celebritynetworth.com/richest-celebrities/rachel-maddow-net-worth/*.

307 Clarence, "Chris Matthews Biography," *ArticleBio*, January 16, 2017, accessed December 13, 2018, *https://articlebio.com/chris-matthews*.

308 Tom Risen, "Brian Williams, MSNBC Seek Redemption in Breaking News," *U.S. News & World Report*, March 25, 2016, accessed December 13, 2018, *https://www.usnews.com/news/articles/2016-03-25/brian-williams-msnbc-seek-redemption-in-breaking-news*.

309 "Joe Scarborough Net Worth, Salary, Age," *WikicelebInfo*, accessed December 13, 2018, *https://wikicelebinfo.com/joe-scarborough-net-worth-salary-age/*.

310 "Mika Brzezinski's Wiki Type Bio including Net Worth, Salary and Age," *WikicelebInfo*, accessed December 13, 2018, *https://wikicelebinfo.com/ mika-brzezinski-wiki-bio-net-worth-salary-age/*.

311 Emmie Martin, "Here's How Much the Average American Earns at Every Age," *CNBC*, August 24, 2017, accessed December 13, 2018, *https://www.cnbc.com/2017/08/24/how-much-americans-earn-at-every-age.html*.

312 "Lester Holt Wife, Son, Parents, Family, Salary, Ethnicity, Age, Height," *Heightline*, accessed December 13, 2018, *https:// heightline.com/lester-holt-wife-salary-height/*.

ACKNOWLEDGMENTS

I am extremely grateful to everyone who made.the publication of this book, my first, possible. A special thank you to Reilly O'Neal, owner of *Big League Politics,* and my friend and agent, Peter Van Voorhis for helping to get the ball rolling on this project. Thank you to Bombardier Books and Post Hill Press for affording me the opportunity to make the publication of this book a reality. Finally, thank you to my family and friends who have encouraged me throughout this incredible experience.

ABOUT THE AUTHOR

Peter D'Abrosca is an investigative reporter and conservative commentator. Originally from the great state of Rhode Island, he is a proud law school dropout whose work has been featured in NewsBusters, The Geller Report, and on DRUDGE. He does most of his daily reporting for *Big League Politics*.